F-22 Raptor

Written by Lou Drendel

In Action®

Squadron/Signal Publications®

Art by Lou Drendel

(Front Cover) With afterburners cooking, and high-G vapor pouring over the inboard wing surfaces, an F-22 Raptor of the 1st Fighter Wing turns towards its prey. The F-22 achieved Initial Operational Capability [IOC] on 15 December 2005. The first operational Raptors were assigned to the 27th Fighter Squadron, with 12 Raptors assigned.

(Back Cover) A Raptor launches a pair of GBU-31 Joint Direct Attack Munitions (JDAM) from its main weapons bay. In air-to-ground mode, the F-22 is able to attack targets from standoff ranges of 15 to 25 miles. The GPS-guided JDAMs will home in on their target in deadly silent accuracy.

About the In Action® Series

In Action® books, despite the title of the genre, are books that trace the development of a single type of aircraft, armored vehicle, or ship from prototype to the final production variant. Experimental or "one-off" variants can also be included. Our first *In Action*® book was printed in 1971.

ISBN 978-0-89747-627-0

Proudly printed in the U.S.A.

1115 Crowley Drive, Carrollton, TX 75006-1312 U.S.A.

Military/Combat Photographs and Snapshots

If you have any photos of aircraft, armor, soldiers, or ships of any nation, particularly wartime snapshots, why not share them with us and help make Squadron/Signal's books all the more interesting and complete in the future? Any photograph sent to us will be copied and returned. Electronic images are preferred. The donor will be fully credited for any photos used. Please send them to:

Squadron/Signal Publications
1115 Crowley Drive
Carrollton, TX 75006-1312 U.S.A.
www.SquadronSignalPublications.com

(Title Page) The dictionary defines the raptor as a bird of prey, e.g., an eagle, hawk, falcon, or owl. The origin is late Middle English, from Latin, literally "plunderer." As the most deadly aerial predator in history, the F-22 Raptor is aptly named.

Acknowledgments

I am indebted to several individuals whose generosity have made this book possible. Eric Hehs, Editor of *Code One* Magazine, provided much of the photography in this book. Long-time friend and contributor John Gourley was quick to answer my request for photos. The websites defense.gov and af.mil were also gold mines of information and photographs.

Introduction

What the F-15 was to the last quarter of the 20th Century, the F-22 is to the first half of the 21st century. The F-15 Eagle was the most dominating air-to-air fighter in history. It has never been bested in aerial combat. The Eagle has an air-to-air record of 104 kills to 0 losses in air combat, and no air-superiority version of the F-15 Eagle has ever been shot down by enemy forces.

It is said that generals plan to fight the last war, and the F-15 was designed to address the air superiority deficiencies of the Vietnam War. As such, it has been an unqualified success, but the F-15 is aging, both technologically and in airframe fatigue life span.

The F-22 was planned to address the anticipated shortcomings of the F-15 when it was matched against several advanced designs from Russian and European consortia. Current Russian fighters such as the MiG-29 and Su-27 are technologically equal to the F-15. The French Rafale, the Eurofighter 2000, and the Russian Su-35 now being produced will surpass the F-15's performance.

In addition to the air-to-air threat to the F-15's dominance, many countries are already challenging U.S. access to their airspace by deploying relatively cheap, yet sophisticated, surface-to-air missile systems.

The need for an advanced, manned fighter was never more critical for the United States to maintain the air supremacy won by the F-15. The F-22 Raptor more than fulfills that need. It is a quantum leap forward in air supremacy capability, incorporating the most advanced avionics, propulsion, stealth, and aerodynamic technologies in the world. No other fighter on earth can match the performance of the Raptor in terms of propulsion, aerodynamics, and data-processing capability.

Unfortunately, at the time of writing, Raptor production has been capped at 187 units by the Barack Obama Administration. While this decision saves money in the short term, it creates a very big potential shortage of air superiority assets if the United States Air Force (USAF) needs to defend air space against a sophisticated adversary.

An F-15E Strike Eagle flies over Afghanistan. The F-15E's primary role in Afghanistan is to provide close-air support for ground troops, but its original mission of long-range strike will be more ably performed by the Raptor. (USAF / Staff Sgt. Aaron Allmon)

An F-16D of the Air Force Test Center at Edwards AFB, California, flies chase on a test Raptor during controllability testing. The F-22 will act as a force multiplier because of its enhanced capabilities, enabling it to augment or supplant the F-16. (Lockheed Martin)

Lockheed Martin's Joint Strike Fighter, the X-35C, is scheduled to replace the F-16 as the primary light strike fighter. It is a contemporary of the Raptor, though less sophisticated. (Lockheed Martin)

Lt Col James Hecker, the 27th Fighter Squadron commander, delivers the first operational F/A-22 Raptor to its permanent home at Langley Air Force Base, Virginia, on 12 May 2005. Tail number 4042 marks the first of 26 Raptors to be delivered to the 27th Fighter Squadron. Capt David Elliot and Maj Charles Corcoran, also assigned to the 27th Fighter Squadron, accompanied the Raptor in an F-15D during its delivery. (USAF / TSgt Ben Bloker)

Genesis

The genesis of the Raptor can be traced to a Tactical Air Command (TAC) study known as TAC-85 undertaken in the early 1970s. In 1969-70, TAC-85 began inquiring into what the USAF fighter of the next century would look like. "Look like" went far beyond the physical appearance of the 21st-century fighter, and it resulted in the issuance of a Concept of Operations in 1971 for the Advanced Tactical Fighter (ATF).

In 1971, the ATF concept was rather nebulous, and since the majority of USAF funding and effort concentrated on making the F-16, F-15, and A-10 operational realities, there were very few studies. What studies there were led the USAF Systems Command to develop a plan to build two sets of ATF prototype by the early 1980s, but the lack of dedicated funding meant that plan would languish unrealized for several years.

Defense doctrine in the 1970s was oriented in the direction of fighting an all-out conventional war with the large, identifiable ground and air forces of the Soviet bloc. The USAF aircraft of the day were dedicated to shooting down swarms of attacking aircraft. The F-15 was the tip of this spear, with its long-range radar and sophisticated air-to-air missiles. The F-16, originally designed as a lightweight point interceptor, *à la* the MiG-21, would out maneuver and destroy its visual-flight-rule (VFR) adversaries, while the rugged but slow A-10 would slug it out with hordes of enemy armor. Stealth was a closely guarded and esoteric technology, and the concept of "owning the night" was just beginning to become a major objective.

By 1978, the ATF concept had become two projects. The Enhanced Tactical Fighter (ETF) would be developed first. The Advanced Tactical Attack System (ATAS) would be developed more slowly in order to take advantage of the progressive development of new weapons and technologies.

Since USAF planners felt confident in the ability of the F-15/F-16 duo to meet known air superiority threats, they concentrated on the ground-attack mission. The emergence of the MiG-29, Su-27, and the MiG-31 disabused USAF of the single mission development track and, in April of 1980, the ETF project was discontinued. The ATAS project was redesignated the Advanced Tactical Fighter (ATF), with air-to-air and air-to-ground roles combined in the same airplane. An adjunct study into the possibility of incorporating Short Take-Off and Landing (STOL) capability was added to the project.

The initial Request For Information (RFI) for the ATF was issued to industry in June of 1981. Invited to submit bids were nine aerospace companies: Boeing, Fairchild, General Dynamics, Grumman, Lockheed, LTV, McDonnell Douglas, Northrop, and North American Rockwell. An RFI for the engine was issued in July. The RFI only specified the mission in the vaguest terms. USAF waited for the industry brainstorming to come up with more defined design and capability parameters.

Seven of the nine companies responded to the RFI. By October 1982, the USAF had decided that supercruise capability was a requirement for the future ATF. (The term "supercruise" refers to the ability of the aircraft to cruise at supersonic speeds without the use of afterburner. It was first used by the so-called "Fighter Mafia" of Col. John Boyd, Pierre Sprey and Col. Everest Riccioni, the designers of the F-16.).

USAF planners focused on confronting the Soviet bloc and its anticipated surge through central Europe in a World War III scenario. Their worries about the vulnerability of current fighters to the integrated air defenses of such a potential enemy led them to require the ATF to be able to fly an entire mission over enemy territory at supersonic speeds. The STOL feature was thought necessary to allow continued operations from damaged runways.

The F-117, the first operational aircraft to rely on stealth for defense, was well along the development pipeline by the early 1980s. The F-15E Strike Eagle was becoming operational, the F-16 had been extensively modified and developed to perform the air-to-ground mission, and the F-111 would probably remain an effective deep penetrator for several more years. Given all of the above, USAF shifted the emphasis of ATF to air-to-air.

The best-case scenario was that the ATF would start entering service in the late 1990s, and would be the primary fighter in service with the USAF at the dawn of the 21st Century. A meeting of USAF planners and U.S. fighter manufacturers in 1982 resulted in an agreement on ATF specifications that included a range of 600 to 800 miles, a maximum takeoff weight in ground attack configuration of 80,000 pounds, supercruise capability, and 2,000-foot runway STOL performance. This agreement resulted in the issuance of a Request for Proposals for the Concept Definition Investigation (RFPCDI) to the industry in late 1982. The final request for proposals (RFP) for the CDI phase was finalized the following May. Remarkably, and in spite of an election year announcement by President Jimmy Carter (hoping to save his job) that the U.S. had or was close to having technology that would render aircraft invisible to radar, the very engineers working on the ATF were not considering what would come to be known as "Stealth" technology. Concept definition contracts were issued to Boeing, General Dynamics, Lockheed, McDonnell Douglas, Northrop, and Rockwell in September 1983.

The Advanced Tactical Fighter Statement of Operational Need (ATFSON) in November 1984 detailed the projected deficiencies of the current generation of fighters. This statement resulted in Congressional funding and approval for the ATF in 1985.

The RFP for the ATF was issued in July 1986. In October, the Phase I Demonstration/Validation program was initiated, and the F-22's Key Performance Parameters were established. They were then documented in the System Operational Requirements document in 1987.

In October 1986, the teams of Lockheed, Boeing, General Dynamics and Northrop, McDonnell-Douglas were selected for the initial demonstration validation phase fly off between the YF-22 and YF-23. (In an acknowledgement of the joint air-to-air/ground attack mission, the projected operation designation was to be "F/A- ," *à la* the F/A-18 Hornet.) The rollout of the prototypes was scheduled for mid-1989. Both ATF prototypes would carry approximately twice the internal fuel of the F-15, were 10% larger had about 50% more wing area and 30% more combat weight. The additional fuel and supercruise capability made for impressive deep interdiction potential.

A four-and-a-half-year demonstration/validation (dem/val) program examined the design, construction, and flight testing of two YF-22 prototypes, which flew with the civil registrations of N22YF and N22YX. The registrations identified the two prototype engines, the General Electric YF120 in the former and the Pratt & Whitney YF119 in the latter.

A parallel engine development program, known as the Joint Advanced Fighter Engine (JAFE) was on-going during the ATF selection process. USAF released its Request For Proposals (RFP) for the development of the engines for the ATF in May 1983. Specifications called for a self-starting engine, with autonomous ground check-out equipment, high thrust-to-weight ratios and high reliability.

In September, Pratt & Whitney and General Electric received contracts to design and build engines for the ATF. The Pratt & Whitney manufacturer designation was the PW5000, and F119 by the Air Force. The General Electric engine carried a GE37 company label and F120 Air Force identifier. The engines were to be interchangeable in the ATF airframe, making either applicable to the ATF. On-going evaluations would determine which manufacturer would build the production ATF engines.

The AFTF demonstration evaluation program was completed in December 1990. The work was performed at the facilities of Boeing in Seattle, Washington; Lockheed in Burbank, California; and General Dynamics in Fort Worth, Texas. The General Dynamics facility was coincidentally an aircraft manufacturing plant that built such famed types as the B-24, B-36, and F-16. The YF-22 prototypes were assembled in Lockheed's famed "Skunkworks" Palmdale, California, facility and made their first flights from there. Lockheed's program management and aircraft assembly operations subsequently moved

The finalists fly together. The Lockheed-Boeing-General Dynamics YF-22 and Northrop-McDonnell Douglas YF-23 never actually competed in a competitive fly-off. (USAF)

The YF-22 is seen on an early test flight. The civilian registration for this prototype was N22YF. It rolled out of the Palmdale plant on 29 September 1990 and made its first flight to Edwards AFB, California, the same day. (USAF)

The design of the Northrop/McDonnell Douglas YF-23 Black Widow II prototype, now displayed at the National Museum of the United States Air Force, Wright-Patterson AFB, Ohio, was a radical departure from conventional design. The unusual shape increased maneuverability and generated high top speeds. The similar angles on all flying surfaces increased stealth characteristics, and also increased instability and maneuverability. The very instability which enhanced maneuverability also dictated computer-controlled fly-by-wire. (USAF)

Some flight testing of the F/A-22 radar was conducted aboard a modified Boeing 757. The test bed consisted of a Raptor forward fuselage installed on the 757's forward pressure bulkhead. Electronic warfare (EW) and communication, navigation, and identification (CNI) sensors were mounted directly on the sensor wing, which was designed to simulate the sensor positioning found on the F-22's wings. (Boeing)

to Marietta, Georgia, for the Engineering and Manufacturing Development (EMD) and production phases.

The System Operational Requirements were updated in March 1991. At the same time, the Advanced Tactical Fighter Full-Scale Development Environmental Assessment was prepared. Full-Scale Development was eventually redesignated as EMD.

In August 1991, the YF-22 with the F-119 engine was declared the winner. According to the Air Force, the F-22 was a better design for maintainability, greater potential for future development, and slightly lower cost. Secretary of the Air Force Donald B. Rice stated that the choice was based on confidence in the ability of the Lockheed team and Pratt & Whitney to produce the aircraft and its engine at projected costs. Emphasizing the importance of the Lockheed team's management and production plans, he denied that either prototype was significantly more maneuverable or stealthy.

The two designs were different enough in size and appearance to generate the inevitable largely uninformed charges of bias towards Lockheed based on nothing more than conspiracy theory. Since the technology was still very secret, no performance figures were published, and there was no head-to-head flyoff. Evaluating pilots did not fly both airplanes and Northrop did not protest its loss too strenuously.

The F-22 passed milestone II in 1991. The System Operational Requirements document was validated by the Air Force and the Department of Defense (DOD) during the 1991 Advanced Tactical Fighter (ATF) Milestone II review. USAF announced a plan to acquire 648 F-22 operational aircraft at a cost of $86.6 billion. After the Bottom Up Review, the planned quantity of F-22s was reduced to 442 at an estimated cost of $71.6 billion in September 1993.

F-22 Design

The initial Lockheed ATF design had a forward fuselage that had a diamond-shaped cross-section, merged into a pentagonal mid-fuselage, and a tapered flat rear fuselage. The body shape was designed with large flat sides, much like the "faceting" philosophy that had been so effective in making the F-117A stealthy. Unlike the F-117, the facet breaks are were not as sharp and there were fewer of them. Curved surfaces were used on the aerodynamic surfaces as well as above and below the fuselage. The use of curved surfaces was made possible using Cray supercomputer simulations of the radar reflectivity of various geometries. (The Cray computer, which became available in the 1980s, allowed aerodynamic breakthroughs, including generation of vortices which enhance maneuverability at high angles of attack, while also mitigating the effects of these vortices on control surfaces.)

Square air intakes flanked a short, smoothly tapered nose, which contains the cockpit and avionics. The external appearance, dictated by the use of Cray supercomputers, maximizes aerodynamic efficiency and enhanced low-observabilty, also known as "Stealth." The speed brake is located on the top of the fuselage between the two vertical tails, *à la* the F-15. As with the other doors on the Raptor, the speed brake has serrated edges to diminish radar returns.

Variable-geometry intake ramps are incompatible with stealthy design because of their shape, and the air intakes of the Raptor are fixed-geometry. The engine air intakes are curved inwards and upwards, which shields the face of the engines from illumination by enemy radars While the YF-22 prototype was about the same size as an F-15, it was heavier, weighing in at 62,000 pounds clean. Despite their similar sizes, in an amazing validation of the computer design, it is estimated that the radar cross-section of the YF-22A is approximately 100 times smaller than that of the F-15. While it is true that some of the Raptor's stealth is achieved by the application of radar-absorbing materials (RAM), RAM is far less prevalent on the F-22 than it is on the airframe of the F-117 "Nighthawk," also known as "Stealth Fighter."

The Raptor's two-shock inlets have ramp angles that were designed for maximum efficiency at Mach 1.5, enhancing Super Cruise capability. Spill doors mounted immediately behind the top lip dump excess air from the inlet at low speeds and low power settings. The intake design enhances low airflow distortion. They are offset from the fuselage by several inches for better boundary layer air control. The intake tunnels which route air to the engines are S-shaped, which shield the face of the engines from Radar beams. A pair of auxiliary blow-in inlets above the body just forward of the vertical fins provide the engines with extra air for starting and takeoff.

The wing is a diamond-shaped, similar to a delta wing. The wings are swept 48° at the leading edge, with close to straight trailing edge, and a small tip chord. The sharp taper reduces the bending loads across the wing since most of the lift is generated close to the root. The wing root chord at the fuselage centerline is 34 feet 6 inches, and the wing tip chord is 4 feet 2 1/2 inches. The wing has no twist or pronounced camber, and there are no canards or leading-edge root extensions.

The wing is fitted with full-span leading edge flaps. The trailing edge has large plain flaps inboard and smaller, tapered flaperons outboard. All of the wing surfaces droop at low speed to reduce takeoff and landing runs.

The Raptor has eight fuel tanks, including one (F-1) in the forward fuselage behind the pilot's ejection seat. Additional tanks are located in the fuselage and the wings. The F-22 uses JP-8, a naphthalene-based fuel with a relatively high flash point. It is equipped with a single-point ground fueling point. It can be refueled without ground power. The F-22 also has an air refueling receptacle on the top side of the fuselage, directly behind the cockpit. The refueling receptacle is covered by two butterfly doors that have integral low-voltage lights to aid in night refueling.

The F-22 also has an On-Board Inert Gas Generation System (OBIGGS) that pressurizes the fuel tanks with nitrogen as the fuel is depleted. JP-8 is not as explosive as the fumes are. By filling the tanks with inert nitrogen as the fuel is used, fumes are suppressed, and the chances of an explosion, are greatly reduced.

The vertical tails of the F-22 are canted outward at 27°. The large vertical tails mask thermal images of the Raptor's engine-exhaust areas and also block infrared search scans from all but the rear and high elevation angles. They are located well forward of the rear of the aircraft, and are 70 percent larger than those of the F-15. Vortexes from the wing were expected to produce heavy stress on the tails, so designers decided to forego an all-flying vertical tail. Instead, there are two fixed vertical stabilizers with moveable rudders. The rudders are about a third of the total tail area.

Two F119-PW-100 advanced-technology afterburning jet engines power the Raptor. It is the most powerful fighter jet engine ever designed, with a maximum thrust of 39,000 pounds. The F-119 has a three-stage fan, a six-stage compressor and single-stage low- and high-pressure turbines. The fan disks and blades are one-piece components. (Lockheed Martin)

Stealth is one of the Raptor's primary attributes. In order to achieve this, all internal and external metal areas are coated with radar absorbent materials (RAM) and with radar absorbent paint (RAP). When the first F-117A was flown, the RAP was expensive to apply and came off easily, which contributed to the F-117's exceedingly high maintenance man hours per flight hour number of 147. (Later improvements got this down to 50.) Landing gear, weapons stowage, blow-in intakes, maintenance access, etc) doors created problem for designers whose mandate included achievement of low observability. Serrated edges were added to the doors to reflect radar returns away from radar return receivers. Intake and cooling vents which must remain open at all times are covered with a low-observable wire mesh to prevent enemy radar emissions from penetrating.

There are over 30,000 self-tests in the Raptor, making it the most easily maintained modern aircraft ever built. Maintainers don't have to spend inordinate amounts of time tracing the source of problems. The tests pinpoint faults immediately. In comparison to the F-15, the F-22 will require half the maintenance man hours per flight hour, which means twice as many consecutive sorties and only two thirds the turn-around time between sorties. Contributing to this capability is the Raptor's On-Board Oxygen Generating System (OBOGS), which provides oxygen to the pilot, eliminating the need for ground-based liquid oxygen (LOX) equipment. The Sortie turnaround rate is enhanced by the Raptor's shortened Integrated Combat Turn (ICT), where the F-22 is refueled, rearmed, and sent back into combat. The F-22's quicker ICT is made possible because of simultaneous gun ammunition and missile reloading, a process that normally goes in sequence only. The Raptor has single-point refueling and a single-point consumables (oil, chaff, flares, etc.) status check point. It also has hydraulic extend and retract missile launchers, which means that there are no pyrotechnics to be concerned with while the aircraft is being turned. The F-22 has an Auxiliary Power Unit (APU), so there is no need for a ground power cart. It only takes four simple steps to take the aircraft from cold on the ramp to engines running.

The operational F-22 was required to achieve 12.0 direct maintenance man-hours per flight hour (DMMH/FH) at system maturity. (Defined to be when the F-22 fleet has accumulated 100,000 flight hours.) The F-22 achieved 18.1 DMMH/FH in 2008, followed by 10.5 DMMH/FH in 2009. System maturity is projected for late 2010. (As this is written in late 2009, the Raptor fleet has exceeded 50,000 flight hours.) The effectiveness of the Raptor maintenance program can be judged by what Northrop had promised for its F-5 Freedom Fighter, a 3rd generation jet, billed as a lightweight, simple export fighter in the 1960s. Northrop projected 22 hours DMMH/FH for their visual-flight-rules (VFR)-only fighter!

Even more startling are the DMMH/FH numbers for Iranian F-4 Phantoms, which are reported to require 135 hours of maintenance for every flight hour! This may be an extreme example, since the Iranian Phantom is a 3rd generation jet fighter, operated by marginally trained, marginally motivated personnel with limited support. However, it does highlight the differences between jet fighters that are potential adversaries.

4th Generation fighters, such as the F-14, F-15, and F-16 have reported DMMH/FH numbers of 24, 22, and 19, respectively. The current DMMH/FH of the Raptor fleet (as of late 2009) is 10.5. Other aircraft which feature stealth characteristics, such as the F-117 and B-2 are 45 and 124 DMMH/FH, respectively.

At the heart of the F-22 are the Pratt & Whitney F119-PW-100 turbofan engines. The F-119 is the only operational fifth generation fighter engine today, and is the most advanced production engine in the world. It combines stealth technologies and vectored thrust with high thrust-to-weight performance, which provides unprecedented maneuverability and survivability. The two F119 engines which power the F-22 Raptor give it "Supercruise" capability. Another of the F119 engine features is its unique two-dimensional pitch vectoring exhaust nozzle. This convergent/divergent nozzle vectors thrust as much as 20° up or down. Nozzle position management is integrated with the F-22 flight control system and is automatically regulated by the Full-Authority Digital Electronic Control (FADEC), as are hundreds of other engine and aircraft operating parameters. The FADEC also features advanced diagnostics and on-condition management capability for maintenance awareness, autonomic logistics support and automatic field and test data processing.

The F119 has a three-stage integrally bladed fan that is powered by a single-stage low-pressure turbine. The engine's counter-rotating core has an aerodynamically efficient six-stage compressor driven by a single-stage high-pressure turbine featuring the latest single-crystal superalloy blades and advanced cooling technologies. The high-pressure compressor features advanced airfoil aerodynamics and integrally bladed rotor disks for ensured durability. The F-119 produces 35,000 lbs. of thrust, a 40% increase over the F-100 engines which power the F-15 Eagle.

Traditional aircraft materials such as aluminum and steel only account for about 20%

One of the two YF-22 prototypes lifts off from Edwards AFB, California, during the test program. The YF-22s tested both the Pratt & Whitney F-119 engines and the General Electric F-120 engines. The P&W F-119 ultimately won the contract for the F-22. (Lockheed Martin)

of the Raptor's weight. Titanium is 42%, while composites are 24%. Both are stronger and lighter than traditional materials, and they offer more protection from corrosion. Titanium offers higher temperature resistance, which is an important consideration because of the F-22's supercruise capability.

The F-22 is the first aircraft to employ Resin Transfer Molding (RTM) of composite parts. RTM is a method of fabrication designed for fabricating complex shaped details on a production line to tight dimensional tolerances.

While large composite parts are traditionally formed by applying and pressurizing hundreds of layers of fabric that contain a pre-embedded resin, then curing them in an autoclave, which is a very time consuming and labor intensive process.

RTM uses fibrous "pre-forms" that are shaped under vacuum from stacks of fabric and placed in metal tooling of the shape of the part, which is then injected with heated resin under pressure. It is the ideal process for consistency and cost-savings.

RTM is used to fabricate more than 400 parts for the F-22's structure ranging from inlet lip edges to load-bearing sine-wave spars in the fighter's wings. It has reduced the cost of wing spars by 20 percent and has cut in half the number of reinforcement parts needed for installing the spars in the wings.

Another F-22 manufacturing automated process is electron beam (EB) welding, which results in lighter-weight titanium assemblies for the aft fuselage. EB welding takes place in a vacuum chamber and uses a stream of electrons to weld titanium parts together.

Performing the welding in a vacuum prevents exposure to oxygen, which can create an undesirably brittle surface. Electron beam welding is able to weld thick titanium parts much more efficiently and to a higher standard than other methods. Electron beam welding reduces the need for fasteners in some fuselage components by as much as 75%. This reduces weight and simplifies the assembly process.

The F-22's cockpit is "all-glass," meaning that there are no traditional round dial gauges, which have come to be known as "steam gages" in pilot parlance. (This in reference to their antiquated nature.) The Raptor cockpit is designed to fit the central 99 percent of the Air Force pilot population, and it is the first baseline "night vision goggle" compatible cockpit. Anticipating the next big thing in tactical aircraft cockpits, there is growth capability for helmet-mounted systems. The $120,00 canopy is the largest piece of polycarbonate formed in the world with the best high quality optics for compatibility with helmet-mounted systems. The F-22 has an improved version of the reliable ACES II ejection seat and a new pilot personal equipment and life support kit.

The GEC-built Head-Up Display (HUD) features a 30° horizontally by 25° vertically field of view. The HUD serves as the primary flight instrument for the pilot. (Meaning that all pertinent information is displayed on the HUD, eliminating the need for the pilot to go "heads-down" to scan instruments.)

The Integrated Control Panel (ICP) is the primary means for manual pilot data entry for communications, navigation, and autopilot data. The ICP is located under the glareshield and HUD, at the center top of the instrument panel. The keypad entry system has some double click functions, much like a computer mouse for rapid pilot access/use.

There are six liquid crystal display (LCD) panels in the cockpit. The LCDs are in full color, but are also fully readable in direct sunlight. Most current aircraft use Cathode Ray Tube (CRT) displays. LCD displays are lower weight and smaller than CRTs. The lower power requirements of CRTs make for more reliability over CRTs. The two Up-Front Displays (UFDs) measure 3"x4" in size and are located to the left and right of the ICP. These display Integrated Caution/Advisory/Warning (ICAW) data, communications/navigation/identification (CNI) data and serve as the Stand-by Flight instrumentation Group and Fuel Quantity Indicator (SFG/FQI).

In most previous tactical aircraft with CRTs, the Stand-by Flight Group was usually presented on "steam gages," which were inconveniently located at the bottom or side of the instrument panel. In the Raptor, the Stand-by Flight Group is presented on an LCD display. It shows the basic information such as attitude, airspeed, and vertical speed, which information the pilot needs to fly the aircraft. The SFG is tied to the last source of power in the aircraft, so if everything else fails, the pilot will still be able to fly the aircraft.

The Primary Multi-Function Display (PMFD) is an eight inch color display which is located in the center of the panel under the ICP. This is the pilot's principal display for aircraft navigation, including showing waypoints and route of flight on a digital map display. It also displays Situation Assessment (SA) or a "God's-eye view" of the entire environment around the airplane. It is a 360 degree, three-dimensional view of the airspace.

The three 6-inch Secondary Multi-Function Displays (SMFDs) are located on either side of the PMFD on the instrument panel and underneath the PMFD between the pilot's knees. They display tactical information and non-tactical information (such as checklists, subsystem status, engine thrust output, and stores management).

Like the F-16, the F-22 has a side-stick controller on the right side of the cockpit, which keeps the area in front of the pilot clear. The two throttles are located on the left console. These are the aircraft's primary flight controls. There is a swing-out, adjustable arm rest for the GEC-built sidesick. Also like the F-16, the stick is force sensitive with a movement of about one-quarter of an inch. The grips of both stick and throttles include buttons and switches that are shape and texture coded to control more than 60 different time-critical functions. (This supports the "Hands-On-Thottle-And-Stick" (HOTAS) concept initiated in 4th generation tactical fighters.) These buttons are used for controlling the offensive and defensive systems as well management of what is displayed on the multi-function displays.

The avionics systems in the Raptor provide a quantum leap in technological combat capabilities, utilizing state-of-the-art processing power. (There are 1.7 million lines of code in the avionics software.) The F-22 has the first integrated avionics suite ever flown in a combat aircraft. The Northrop/Grumman-Texas Instruments APG-77 radar, Lockheed Martin electronic warfare suite and the TRW communications/navigation/IFF subsystems provide integrated Communications, Navigation, Identification Avionics (ICNIA) and Integrated Electronic Warfare System (INEWS) to the pilot.

Avionics in the Raptor have very high-speed integrated circuit (VHSIC) technologies, common modules, and high-speed data buses. They comprise a highly integrated system which frees the pilot to concentrate on the mission, while the system manages the sensors. (In 4th generation fighters, the pilot is tasked with sensor management.) System management includes radar, electronic warfare, and identification sensor data, as well

This production test F-22 reflects significant changes from the YF-22 prototype. The sweep of the wing leading edge was cut from 48° to 42° and the vertical stabilizer area was reduced 20%. The cockpit canopy was moved forward 7 inches, and the engine intakes were moved 14 inches to the rear. The area of the wing and stabilators were increased to improve aerodynamics, strength, and stealth. (Lockheed Martin)

The prototype YF-22 is seen just prior to roll-out. It was equipped with a fully instrumented nose boom for testing purposes. The air-data nose boom fed information on airspeed, pitch, yaw, angle-of-attack, and sideslip to a cockpit-mounted cathode ray tube (CRT) display. The boom is 10 feet long and weighs more than 600 pounds. (Lockheed Martin)

as communication, navigation, weapon, and systems status data. The avionics have a Common Integrated Processor (CIP), which has the equivalent computing power of two Cray supercomputers; shared low-observable antennas; ADA software; expert systems; advanced data fusion-cockpit displays; integrated electronic warfare system (INEWS) technology; integrated communications, navigation, and identification (CNI) avionics technology; and fiber optics data transmission.

The AN/APG-77 radar is the most advanced airborne radar in the world. It is the primary Raptor sensor, and the ground-breaking technologies used add to the overall capabilities of the F-22. It is an active-element, electronically scanned (unlike other airborne radar antennas, it does not move) array that features a separate transmitter and receiver for each of the antenna's several thousand, small radiating elements. Since the antenna does not move, most of the mechanical linkages and motors common to other radars have been eliminated, making the AN/APG-77 lighter and more reliable than other contemporary radars. The antenna is integrated both physically and electromagnetically with the airframe, which provides the frequency agility, low radar cross-section, and wide bandwidth that make the Raptor the most advanced fighter ever built. It gives the pilot detailed information about multiple threats before the enemy radar ever detects the F-22.

Another of the systems which makes the F-22 such a potent fighter is an Inter/Intra-Flight Data Link (IFDL) that allows all F-22s in a flight to share target and system data automatically without verbal communication. The Inter/Intra Flight Data Link allows flight leaders to manage the battlespace more efficiently. With the IFDL, the leader can tell at a glance what his wing mans fuel state is, his weapons remaining, and even the enemy aircraft he has targeted. In the heat of high-speed aerial warfare, quick and accurate decisions are critical to winning and surviving. IFDL allows the F-22 pilot to automatically prioritize and set up in a shoot list of targets with a single button. A "shoot" cue in the HUD alerts the pilot to the selected weapons kill parameters and he fires the weapons. All offensive missile shots can be monitored on the cockpit displays.

The capabilities of the Raptor are forcing tacticians to modify time-honored fighter tactics. The relatively low numbers of Raptors available to commanders can be offset by the capabilities of the F-22 as new tactics evolve.

F-22 Weapons

The primary mission of the Raptor is air-to-air combat to achieve "air dominance," a term that is defined as giving friendly forces the ability to operate over the battlefield unhindered by enemy aircraft. The F-22's primary weapons are the AIM-120C and AIM-9 missiles, and the internal M61A2 20mm cannon.

The M61 has been around since the 1950s. The F-104, F-105, F-106, F-111, F-4, F-15, F-16, F-14, and F/A-18 all have been equipped with the gun. In the Raptor, it is internally mounted on the right side of the aircraft, between the wing and fuselage. It is a fixed-forward firing mount, and to preserve stealthiness, the gun door is hydraulically

The Northrop YF-23 ATF prototype used jet exhausts similar to those found on the B-2 Stealth Bomber. While this enhanced stealth characteristics, it precluded the use of thrust vectoring of the engines. (USAF)

The F-22 exhaust is more conventional than the YF-23, and is articulated for thrust vectoring, which enhances maneuverability, particularly at slow speeds. (USAF / Capt. Dale Greer)

controlled to open when firing the gun, allowing the rounds and blast pressure to clear the muzzle. A 480-round closed loop ammunition feed and storage subsystem is housed internally, under the right wing root/fuselage area for easy upload and download of empty casings. The gun system consists of the M61A2 gun, Linear Linkless Ammunition Handling System (LLAHS), hydraulic drive system, and the gun door/gun port and gas purge system.

The A2 is a lightweight version of the M61A1. Like its predecessor, it is a "Gatling" type gun, with six rotating barrels. It can be set to fire 100 rounds per second. The Raptor carries 480 rounds of ammunition for the M61A2.

The AIM-120C is the latest version of the Advanced Medium-Range Air-to-Air Missile (AMRAAM). AMRAAM was developed to replace the AIM-7 Sparrow. Like the AIM-7, the AIM-120 is radar-guided. Unlike the Sparrow, the AIM-120 provides an all-weather, all-environment launch capability. The "Slammer," as it is known by pilots, gets targeting information from the aircraft systems prior to launch. Once launched, the missile can operate autonomously using its own inertial guidance system and an active radar, giving the F-22 "launch and leave" capability. If necessary, the missile can receive mid-course target updates from the launch aircraft.

The Raptor carries six AIM-120s internally, three in each of the main missile bays, which are covered by two thermoset composite bifold doors that open outward. The missiles are staggered in the bay so fins on adjacent missiles do not interfere with each other when they are launched. They are hydraulically ejected from the bay by LAU-142/A pneudraulic (pneumatic and hydraulic) launchers, (AMRAAM Vertical Eject Launcher, or AVEL). The AVEL is heavy enough (nearly 113 pounds each) to minimize missile movement in the weapons bay. The AVEL has a nine-inch stroke, and ejects the missile out of the bay at more than 25 feet per second with a force of 40Gs at peak acceleration. While conventional missile launchers on other aircraft use an explosive cartridge to eject the missile from the launch aircraft, the AVEL requires no pyrotechnics. The AVEL therefore needs less logistics support than do other launchers. The AIM-120C is 12 feet long, weighs 335 pounds, and costs U.S. taxpayers $400,000. It has true Beyond Visual Range (BVR) capability, with a range of 65 miles, and a top speed of MACH 4.

The Raptor also carries the latest operational version of the venerable AIM-9 Sidewinder missile, which was introduced as early as 1953. The AIM-9M is an all-aspect IR-guided missile that is carried internally in the F-22 side weapons bays. The AIM-9M has an increased ability to defeat infrared countermeasures, and a smokeless rocket motor to make it more difficult for enemy pilots to acquire and defeat the incoming missile. Since guidance depends strictly on the heat signature of the target, the two thermoset composite side bay doors that run the length of the compartment, and are hinged at the top and bottom of the bay, must be opened, and the missile extended on the launch rail before the target can be acquired. The Raptor carries two AIM-9s, one in each of the side bays.

Unlike the F-15C, which the Raptor was designed to replace, the F-22 will carry air-to-ground ordnance. The F-22 carries the 1,000-pound class Joint Direct Attack Munition (JDAM) weapon. The JDAM tail guidance kit contains a GPS receiver and fits on the Mk. 83 1,000-pound-class conventional bomb. The combination of the stealthy F-22 with the precision 15-meter CEP capability of the GBU-32 allows the F-22 pilot to drop the weapon from altitudes of up to 40,000 feet at a range of approximately 15 miles from the target. This height and distance greatly limit the enemy's ability to defend against the Raptor. The F-22 carries the GBU-32 in the aircraft's main weapons bay. A typical combat load consists of two GBU-32s, one inboard in each side of the main weapons bay. This configuration leaves room in the F-22's main weapons bay for two AIM-120C air-to-air missiles. The two AIM-9 Sidewinders in the side weapons bays give the Raptor significant air-to-air combat capability, even when carrying air-to-ground weapons.

In air-to-ground mode, the F-22A can carry two Global Positioning System-aided 250-pound GBU-39/B Small Diameter Bombs in place of two AIM-120s and two AIM-9 missiles in the weapons bays. The Small Diameter Bomb (SDB) (Guided Bomb Unit [GBU]-39/B) gives the F-22A multiple targeting capabilities. The SDB is appropriately named, since it weighs just 250 pounds and has a diameter of only six inches. This size allows more GBU-39s to be loaded into an F-22, thereby increasing the target capabilities of the F-22 by 400 percent. Instead of two JDAMs, the aircraft will carry eight SDBs internally. The small size and weight also give the Raptor an increased stand-off range of 50 nautical miles at 40,000 feet and .95 Mach. The GBU-39A mounting carriage is the BRU-61/A, which fits four bombs on one weapon pylon.

The F-22 has an all-glass cockpit and, unlike fourth generation fighters, which also had glass, it does not have any backup analog instruments. Also shown here is the sidestick control, proven to be ergonomically effective in fighter cockpits. (Lockheed Martin)

A test-configured Raptor conducts a test flight early in the program. The first F-22 completed about 100 flights before the second airplane (Aircraft 4002) took off for the first time in mid-1998. Initial test flights were made over Georgia before the second aircraft was ferried to Edwards AFB, California, to undergo high-angle-of-attack testing and, later, tests of weapon separations from the internal bay. The appearance of the production F-22 Raptor is markedly different from that of the YF-22 prototypes. (Lockheed Martin)

The F-22 cockpit is sized to accommodate the 0.5 percentile to 99.5 percentile pilots, which is the body size of the central 99% of the Air Force pilot population. (USAF /Staff Sgt. Jason Colbert)

The first production F-22 Raptor first took to the air on 7 September 1997. F-22 Chief Test Pilot Paul Metz flew the aircraft from Dobbins Air Reserve Base. Dobbins is adjacent to the Lockheed Martin assembly plant at Marietta, Georgia. Raptor 01 then flew to Edwards AFB, California, for the extensive testing program. (Lockheed Martin)

Raptor 01 with landing gear extended during a test flight. The F-22 landing gear is a Menasco retractable tricycle type, stressed for no-flare landings of up to 3.05m/s downward speed. The nose wheel tire measures 23.5 x 7.5-10 and the two main gear tires measure 37 x 11.5-18. (Lockheed Martin)

Air Force Research Laboratory (AFRL), Wright Patterson Air Force Base, Dayton, Ohio reported that a redesign of the F-22 Raptor turbine engine exhaust case (TEC) from a built-up assembly of sheet metal components to an assembly of fewer investment castings had cut the cost of the TEC by 35% and increased engine durability. The TEC, as shown here, can be diverted to provide thrust vectoring. (Lockheed Martin)

Among the differences between production Raptors and the early test versions are the blade antennas on top and bottom of the fuselage, and the fully instrumented nose probe used to measure angle-of-attack, side-slip, and precise airspeeds. (Lockheed Martin)

The F-22's F119 engine features the first full-production vectoring exhaust in the world. The two-dimensional exhaust vectors thrust 20° up and down for improved aircraft agility. This vectoring raises the aircraft's roll rate by 50%. The exhaust nozzles' shape enhances the F-22's stealthiness. With precision digital controls, the nozzles act like another aircraft flight-control surface. (USAF / Senior Airman Garrett Hothan)

The F-119 engines were subjected to full-scale airframe static tests, including three planned fatigue lifetimes of testing. The F119 can push the F-22 to supersonic speeds above Mach 1.4 without the use of afterburner, (Supercruise), giving the Raptor greater operating range and a stealthier profile. (Lockheed Martin)

The instrumented nose probe on test Raptors provides precise test data on angle-of-attack (AOA) and sideslip readings as well as corresponding airspeed read-outs. (Lockheed Martin)

Like all modern fighters, the pilot's primary instrument scan is through the heads-up-display (HUD) The GEC-built HUD offers a field of view of 30° horizontally by 25° vertically. The F-22's HUD is approximately 4.5 inches tall and uses standardized symbology developed by the Air Force Instrument Flight Center. (USAF)

Technicians check the status of multi-function displays in the cockpit of the #4 test Raptor. The F-22 avionics and software systems are the most advanced ever incorporated in an aircraft. The first aircraft to use integrated radar, weapons management, and electronic warfare systems, the Raptor relieves the pilot of the task of interpreting data from these systems, giving him unprecedented situation awareness. (Lockheed Martin)

Two of the test Raptors out of Edwards AFB, California. The government/contractor integrated test team was composed of personnel from the Air Force Flight Test Center (AFFTC) at Edwards AFB, California; the Air Force Operational Test and Evaluation Center (AFOTEC) from Kirtland AFB, New Mexico; Air Combat Command (ACC), (the ultimate user of the F-22), headquartered at Langley AFB, Virginia; Pratt & Whitney, the F-22 System Program Office (SPO) at Wright Patterson AFB, Ohio; and the Lockheed Martin Boeing team. They were co-located at Edwards in October 1997. (Lockheed Martin)

The number-two Raptor was fitted with an anti-spin recovery parachute system for high angle-of-attack (AOA) testing. If the test pilot could depart controlled flight, but could not recover using conventional control inputs, the recovery parachute was deployed, stabilizing the aircraft in a decelerated nose-down attitude. (Lockheed Martin)

Though the F-22 is dynamically unstable, and therefore capable of great maneuverability, its computer-controlled controls make it nearly impossible for the pilot to depart from controlled flight. The widely expanded performance envelope was explored exhaustively with the test aircraft. (Lockheed Martin)

Camouflage

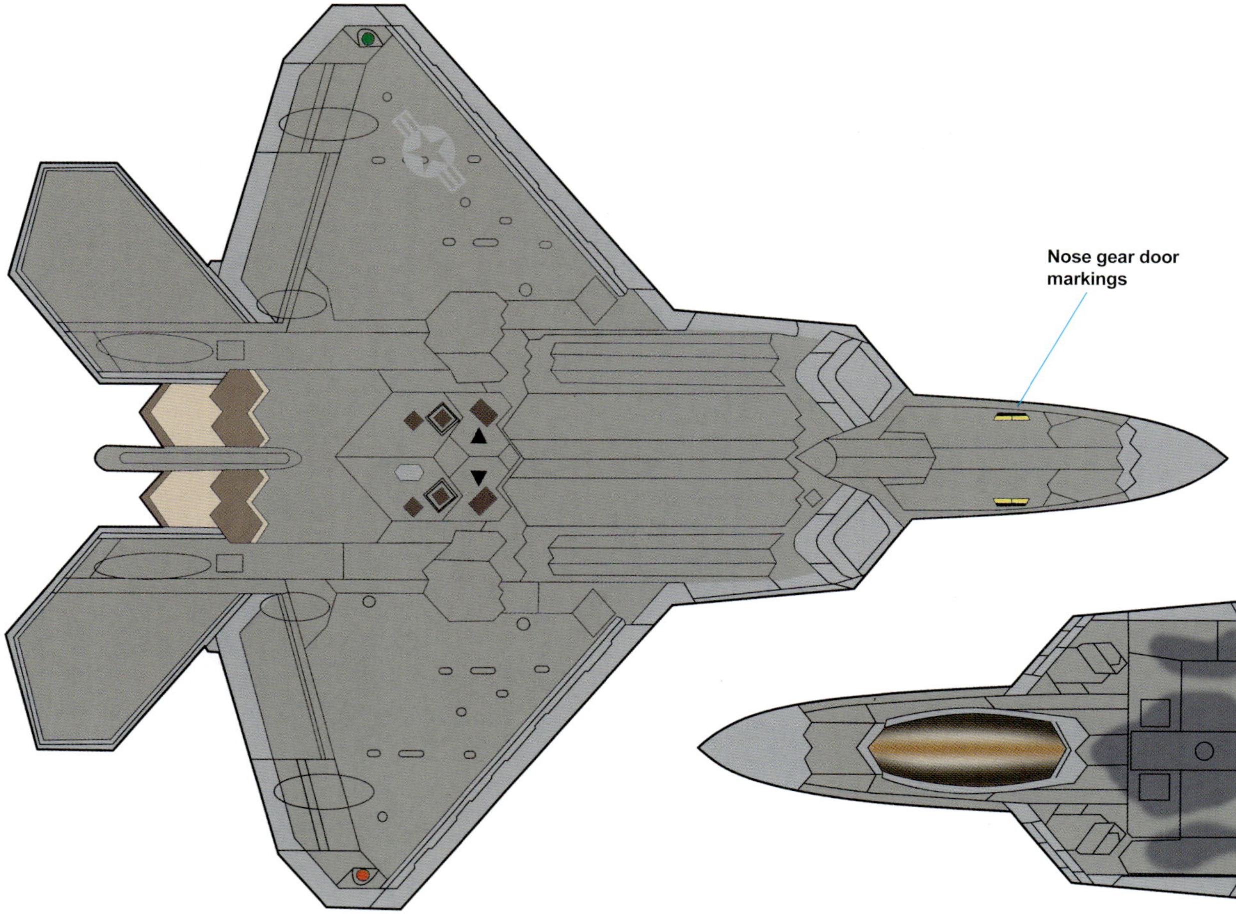

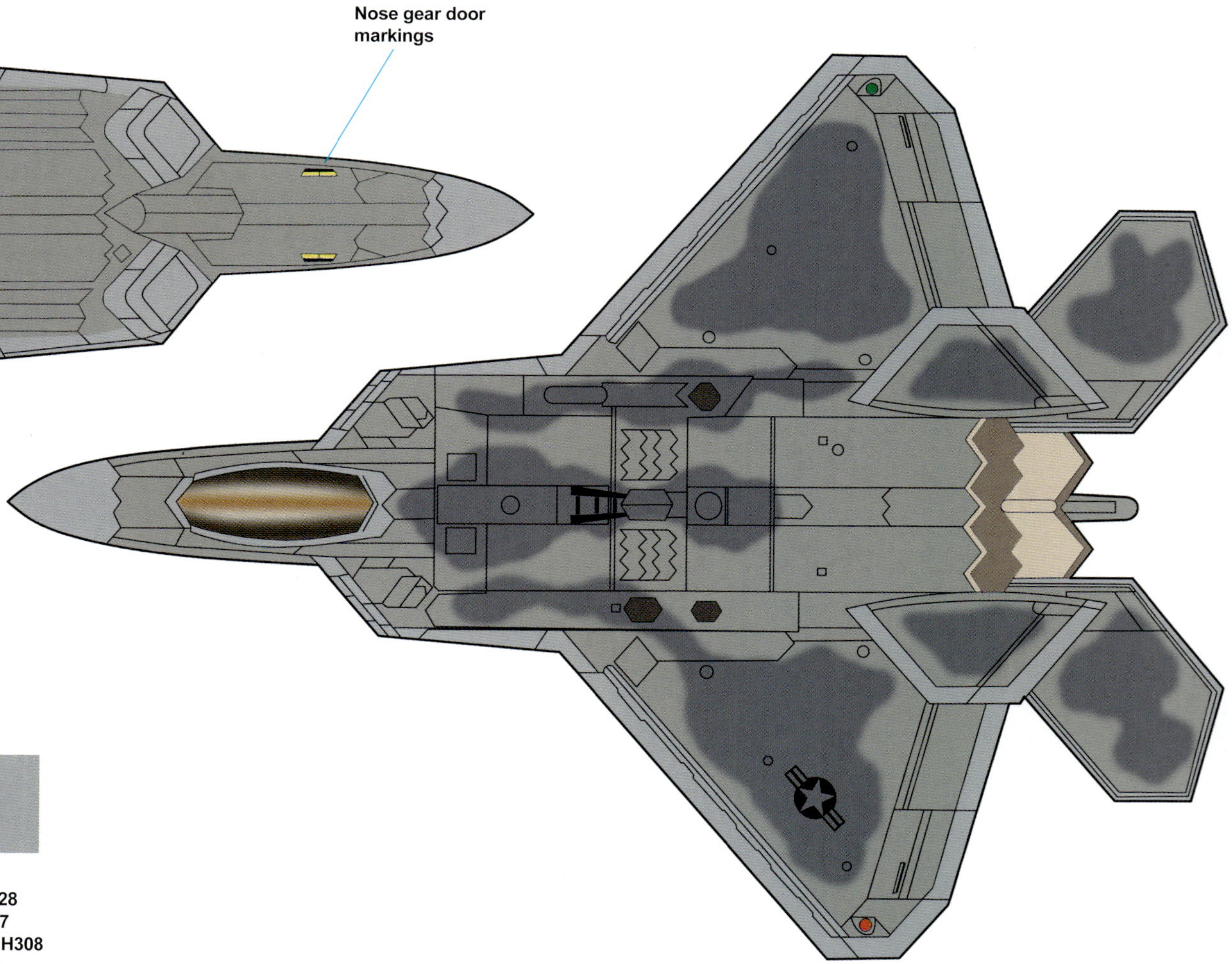

FS36251
Testors MM 1794
Humbrol HU145
Funze Sangyo NA
Xtracolor X132
Xtracrylics XA1132

FS36176
Testors MM 2036
Humbrol NA
Funze Sangyo NA
Xtracolor X157
Xtracrylics XA1157

FS36176
Testors MM 1728
Humbrol HU127
Funze Sangyo H308
Xtracolor X136
Xtracrylics XA1136

The F-22 demonstrates its maneuverability during an airshow demonstration. The Raptor pilot is able to achieve dramatic changes in angle-of-attack without fear of over-G-ing the airplane because of the computer-controlled flight controls. (Lockheed Martin)

The F-22 has an Xar-built air refueling receptacle on the top side of the aircraft in the mid fuselage directly behind the cockpit. It is covered by two butterfly doors that have integral low-voltage lights to help night refueling. Like the landing gear doors, the refueling receptacle doors are speed-limited. If the pilot is in danger of exceeding the limit, an aural warning will sound in his headset. (Lockheed Martin)

The F-22 canopy is the largest monolithic polycarbonate item currently being manufactured. It is resistant to chemical/biological agents and is advertised to protect the pilot from lightning strikes. The two-layer laminate has been tested to withstand a four-pound bird strike at 350 knots. Since 1990, at least 107 military aircraft have been destroyed by bird strikes. (Lockheed Martin)

Final assembly operations for the Raptor take place in the 3.5-million-square-foot B-1 building, which has been in near-continuous use since 1943, at Lockheed Martin Aeronautics Company in Marietta, Georgia. The forward fuselage and canopy are built in Marietta, while the mid-fuselage is built in Fort Worth, and the aft fuselage and wings are built by Boeing in Seattle. (Lockheed Martin)

For quality control, workers may not use their own tools in the F-22's Final Assembly Area at Marietta, seen here in a fish-eye view. All tools are shadowboxed in company-issued toolboxes. Whenever a tool is removed from its slot, it must be replaced with a chit bearing the photograph and number of the employee who removed it. All tools must be accounted for at the end of each shift, after which the boxes are locked until the next shift comes in. This practice keeps tools from being left in the F-22. (Lockheed Martin)

The digital revolution in fighter design means that ground crewmen can monitor all of the Raptor's systems via laptop. The F-22 is designed to allow replacement of electronic components without the use of special platforms or ladders. (Lockheed Martin)

The Raptor training squadron is the 43rd Fighter Squadron at Tyndall AFB, Florida. The twin vertical tails of the F-22 production aircraft are 20% smaller than the prototype YF-22. The prototype's larger rudders were a design feature meant to counter spins. When the spin problem did not materialize during testing, the tails were reduced in size to decrease drag and enhance stealth. (John Gourley)

The shape of the horizontal stabilator on production aircraft was changed to reduce observability, to add structural strength, and for aerodynamic refinement.

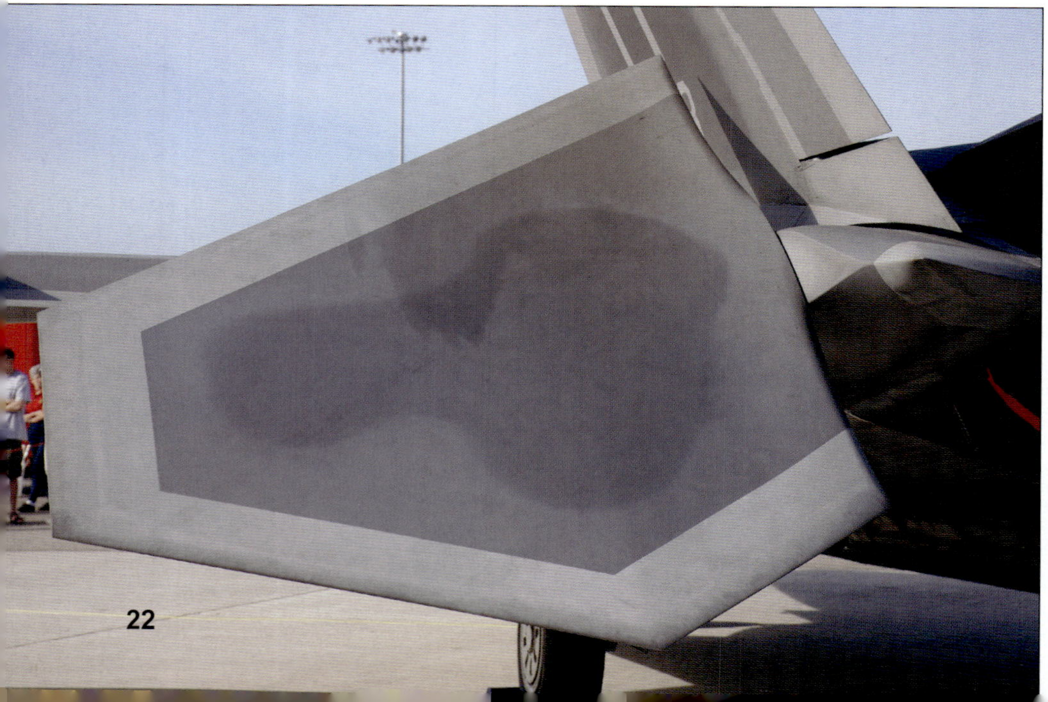

The large, articulated exhaust vanes of the F-119 engines act as speed brakes as well as thrust vectors. The F-22 is the first operational fighter to feature thrust vectoring, which enhances maneuverability and is integrated seamlessly in the Raptor's flight controls.

The Portable Maintenance Aid (PMA) is a 10-lb. hand-held computer that plugs into a receptacle in the wheel well. The PMA is the primary maintenance interface with the aircraft and its systems. It displays Interactive Electronic Technical Manuals (IETMs), can order parts, and fills in maintenance forms. (Lockheed Martin)

These two Raptors belong to the 422nd Test and Evaluation Squadron, which is responsible for developing and testing of new tactics for a wide variety of USAF aircraft. (Lockheed Martin)

On 4 September 2008, an Edwards F-22 Raptor became the first USAF aircraft to refuel in mid-air using an alternative fuel, a 50/50 mix of JP-8 jet fuel and a natural gas-based fuel. Naphthalene-based JP-8 has a relatively high flash point. (Lockheed Martin)

A USAF F-22 Raptor (left) and an F-15 Strike Eagle from the 325th Fighter Wing take part in air-to-air maneuvers over Florida on 22 September 2008. The Raptor has replaced the Eagle in F-22 units but, due to its limited numbers, will not totally supplant F-15s. Eagles and Raptors will share the sky for years to come. (USAF / Master Sgt. Scott Reed)

The F/A-22 Raptor shows its claws during a side weapons bay test at Edwards AFB, California. The F/A-22 is designed to carry two AIM-9M or Sidewinder short-range, heat-seeking air-to-air missiles in its side weapons bays, and will eventually carry the more advanced AIM-9X. (USAF)

Armament

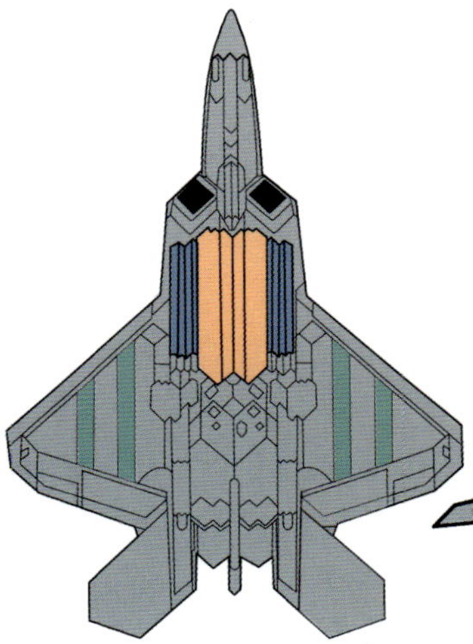

M61A2 Cannon
(480 rounds)
5,000-pound hardpoints
5,000-pound hardpoints

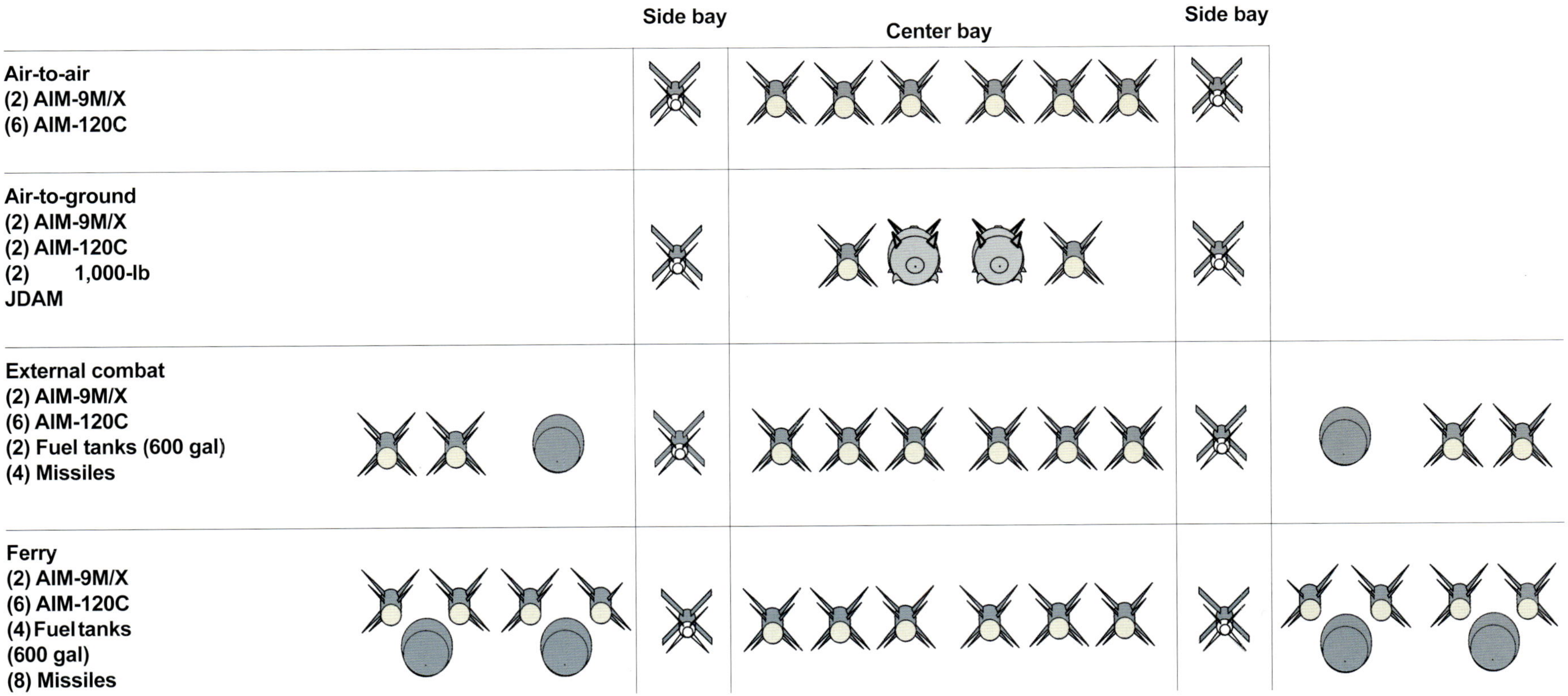
Side bay
Center bay
Side bay
Air-to-air
(2) AIM-9M/X
(6) AIM-120C
Air-to-ground
(2) AIM-9M/X
(2) AIM-120C
(2) 1,000-lb
JDAM
External combat
(2) AIM-9M/X
(6) AIM-120C
(2) Fuel tanks (600 gal)
(4) Missiles
Ferry
(2) AIM-9M/X
(6) AIM-120C
(4) Fuel tanks
(600 gal)
(8) Missiles

A U.S. Air Force weapons loader with the 36th Expeditionary Maintenance Squadron conducts a preflight inspection on an F-22 Raptor aircraft at Andersen Air Force Base, Guam, 2 March 2009. The 90th Fighter Squadron from Elmendorf Air Force Base, Alaska, was completing a three-month deployment there as part of a theater security package. (USAF / Airman 1st Class Courtney Witt)

A weapons loader prepares a GBU-31 joint direct attack munition for a mission at a forward-deployed location. Smart bombs like the JDAM have comprised 80 percent of the munitions used during operation Iraqi Freedom. The GBU-31 is one of the primary air-to-ground weapons carried by the Raptor. (USAF /Staff Sgt. Jessica Kochman)

Airman 1st Class Brett Lewis and Staff Sgts. Christopher Stacklin and Nicholas Lanna, 27th Aircraft Maintenance Unit weapons-load crew members, load a missile onto an F-22A at Langley AFB, Virginia, on 17 April 2009. Squadron finalists are judged quarterly on their accuracy, efficiency, and speed. The light-weight, the AIM-9 is typically loaded by hand in the interest of speed. (USAF / Airman 1st Class Gul Crockett)

Sidewinders are carried on a Lockheed Martin Tactical Aircraft Systems-built LAU-141/A hydraulic Trapeze Launcher. The LAU-141 uses some components from the existing LAU-128/A launcher, which is the wingtip launch rail from an F-16 with a swing out mechanism that extends rapidly. (John Gourley)

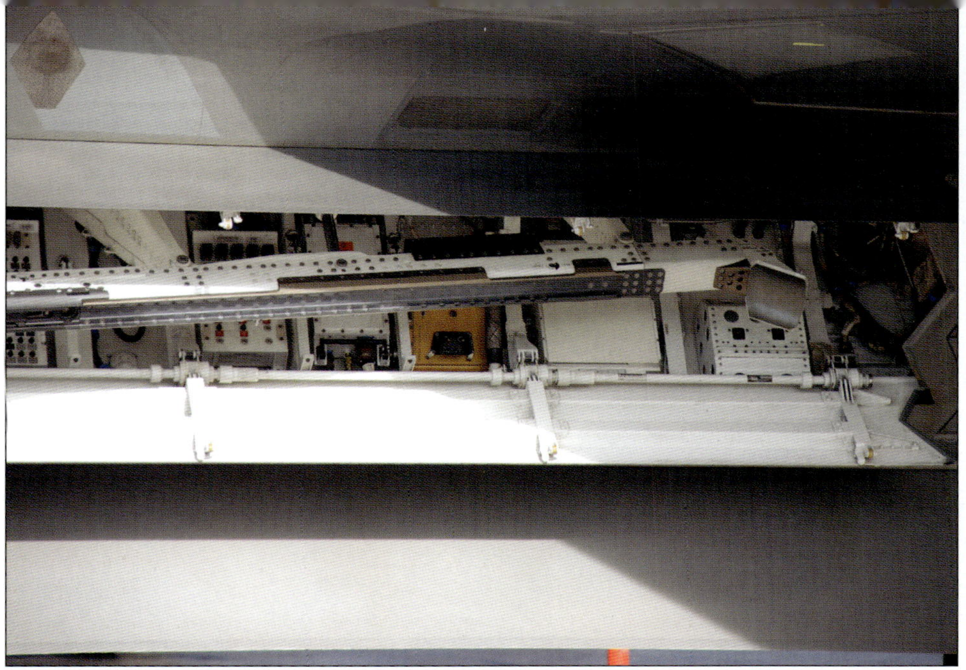

The LAU-141/A is also fitted with a missile motor plume deflector, which prevents damage to the side weapons bay as the missile launches off the rail. Each AIM-9 is loaded by opening the doors, extending the rail, sliding it on the rail, retracting the missile, and closing the doors.

A Tyndall Raptor with all weapons bays doors open. At the 2007 MacDill AFB Open House.

The heat-seeking AIM-9 missile has to acquire the target prior to launch. After the side weapons bay doors open, the Trapeze Launcher, with missile attached, extends to put the missile's seeker out of the bay. As soon as the seeker acquires the target; the missile fires off the rail. The Trapeze Launcher retracts, and the weapons bay doors close.

Side bay doors are open on this F-22 and the AIM-9 is exposed prior to firing in a September 2003 test flight. (Lockheed Martin)

In a 2009 test, F-22A aircraft 4007 flight 686, from Edwards AFB fires a live AIM-9M Sidewinder missile at a drone over the Naval Weapon Test Center range in southern California. The AIM-9M has a no-smoke rocket engine, making it more difficult for enemy pilots to avoid the incoming missile. (Lockheed Martin /Darrin Russell)

Senior Airman Daniel Myers and Staff Sgts. Daphne Jaehn and John Davenport load an AIM-120D Advanced Medium Range Air-to-Air Missile on an F-22A Raptor in preparation for noise and vibration testing at Edwards Air Force Base, Calif. The Airmen are assigned to the base's 412th Aircraft Maintenance Squadron and are with the F-22 Combined Test Force weapons flight. The missiles are loaded from the opposite side of the aircraft AIM-120 Loading in Main Weapons Bay (missiles in the left side of the weapons bay are loaded from the right and visa versa), in order to clear the open main weapons bay doors. The current MJ-1 load vehicle (called a jammer) is used to load the missiles into the F-22. The missiles are staggered in the bay so fins on adjacent missiles do not interfere with each other when they are launched. (USAF / Kevin Robertson)

Airman 1st Class Amber Wagner inspects a practice GBU-32 JDAM after it is loaded onto an F-22 Raptor 14 April 2009 at Elmendorf Air Force Base, Alaska. Airman Wagner, assigned to the 525th Aircraft Maintenance Unit, ensured the JDAM dropped by the 525th Fighter Squadron was successful. The GBU-32 is carried on the inboard launcher, while the outboard launcher would carry an AIM-120 for a combat mission. (USAF / Senior Airman Jonathan Steffen)

A Raptor shows the relative size of its four weapons bays. The large weapons bays carry the GBU-32 JDAM and the AIM-120 AAMRAM, while the smaller side bays carry the AIM-9 AAM. The Raptor can also carry the GBU-39/B Small Diameter Bomb. (Lockheed Martin)

An Edwards Raptor launches a heat-seeking missile countermeasures flare from the bay immediately behind the open side weapons bay. The small appendage on the belly of the F-22 is a camera fitted to record weapons release testing. (Lockheed Martin)

Tech. Sgts. Thomas Harper, David Martens and Steve Breeden load an AIM-9 missile on station 3 of an F-22A during the weapons load competition at the 94th Fighter Squadron on 17 October 2007. This 192nd Air National Guard crew works out of the 94th Aircraft Maintenance Unit. Competitions are held on a quarterly basis and winners compete for the Load Crew of the Year. (USAF / Senior Airman Cecil C. McCloud)

Staff Sgt. Temujin Ching, 477th Aircraft Maintenance Squadron, hooks up the aft closed loop liquid cooling system to an F-22A Raptor. Polyalphaolefin (PAO) is the medium used in the liquid cooling system. The 477th AMXS is the first Reserve F-22 squadron in the Air Force. It is assigned to the Tenth Air Force, and based at Elmendorf AFB, Alaska. (USAF / Senior Airman Garrett Hothan)

4007 Launches an AIM-120 from an LAU-142/A pneudraulic (pneumatic and hydraulic) launcher, also known as an AMRAAM Vertical Eject Launcher (AVEL). Each AVEL weighs113 lbs, and minimizes missile movement in the weapons bay. The AVEL has a nine-inch stroke and ejects the missile out of the bay at more than 25 feet per second with a force of 40 Gs at peak acceleration. Unlike conventional missile launchers on other aircraft, the AVEL requires no pyrotechnics, which means less logistics support. (Lockheed Martin)

A Raptor fires its M-61A2 20mm cannon. When the gun fires, a hydraulically controlled gun door in the wing root area opens up to allow the rounds and blast pressure to clear the muzzle. A 480-round closed-loop ammunition feed and storage subsystem is housed integrally under the right wing root/fuselage for easy ammunition upload and downloading spent casings. (Lockheed Martin)

Staff Sgt. Jason McDonald (left), a weapons-load crew chief, checks his technical orders after loading two joint direct attack munitions onto an F/A-22 Raptor at Hill AFB, Utah, in April 2007. The sergeant and the Raptors, from the 27th Fighter Squadron at Langley Air Force Base, Virginia, deployed here to take part in exercise Combat Hammer. Six different types of aircraft took part in the 86th Fighter Weapons Squadrons Weapons System Evaluation Program. (USAF /Staff Sgt. Samuel Rogers)

Two Aircraft Maintainers from the 27th Fighter Squadron inspect an FA/22 Raptor stealth fighter jet prior to a flight. AIM-9 launchers were not fitted for this early flight from Langley AFB, Virginia. The 27th Fighter Squadron is the oldest squadron in the USAF. (USAF / Staff Sgt. V. Levi Collins)

Maj. Patrick Deconcini, of the 192nd VAANG, assigned to the 94th FS, performs a preflight inspection of an F-22 Raptor at Langley Air Force Base, Virginia. The 94th Fighter Squadron deployed for a Red Flag exercise at Nellis AFB, Nevada. The long-running Red Flag is an air combat training exercise designed to test pilots and air support crews' ability to effectively respond to real-world combat scenarios. This was the first deployment to Red Flag for the 94th FS with F-22s. (USAF / Staff Sgt. Samuel Rogers)

Lt. Col. James Hecker flies over the ramparts of Fort Monroe, Virginia. The colonel, who commands the 27th Fighter Squadron at Langley Air Force Base, Virginia, flew the first of 26 Raptors to his unit in September 2007. (USAF / TSgt Ben Bloker)

Maj. Micah Fesler, a 433rd Weapons Squadron pilot, flies an F-22A “Raptor” from the Lockheed-Martin factory in Marietta, Georgia, to Nellis AFB, Nevada. This Raptor was the first to be delivered to the 57th Wing from Lockheed-Martin, and is used by the U.S. Air Force Weapons School for training of Ph.D.-level instructor pilots. (USAF / TSgt. Phil Landram)

Staff Sgt. Geneva Rumbaugh reviews her checklist after loading a Joint Direct Attack Munition (JDAM) onto an F-22 Raptor. At the same time, Airman 1st Class Justin Baker inspects the JDAM at Elmendorf Air Force Base, Alaska. Sergeant Rumbaugh and Airman Baker are from the 525th Aircraft Maintenance Unit. (USAF / Senior Airman Jonathan Steffen)

Pilots from the 525th Fighter Squadron discuss what to look for when a Joint Direct Attack Munition is loaded onto an F-22 Raptor. The GBU-32 JDAM is based on the 1,000-lb. Mk-83. It becomes a JDAM when INS/GPS guidance is added to the tail of the bomb. Accuracy of the JDAM is within 10 meters, circular error probable (CEP). (USAF / Senior Airman Jonathan Steffen)

A test Raptor demonstrates the F-22 ability to fire its weapons while maneuvering. It has launched an AIM-9 heat-seeking missile at a drone target. The AIM-9 has been in service with USAF since 1956, though the latest version of the venerable design bears little resemblance to the earlier versions. (Lockheed Martin)

The first test Raptor, with afterburners lit, is seen on a low-level fly-by at Edwards AFB, California. Each of the Pratt & Whitney F119-PW-100 turbofan engines develops 35,000 lbs. of thrust in afterburner. It is equipped with a number of advanced technologies, including a three-stage integrally bladed fan, powered by a single-stage low-pressure turbine. The engine's counter-rotating core has an aerodynamically efficient six-stage compressor, driven by a single-stage high-pressure turbine which has single-crystal superalloy blades and advanced cooling technologies. (Lockheed Martin)

Unlike all previous generations of jet fighters, the Raptor achieves its best time to climb performance by simply accelerating to supersonic speed on the deck, and then climbing at supersonic speed. Since no official attempts at breaking existing records have been made, the exact figures on time to climb have not been released. (Lockheed Martin)

Staff Sgt. Chris McKee, Airman 1st Class Daniel Aydelotte, and Senior Airman Johnglenn Gararce, the competing weapons load crew from the 27th Fighter Squadron, carry a missile to an F-22 at Langley AFB, Virginia. The competition for squadron finalists is held annually with the teams being judged on their accuracy, efficiency, and speed. (USAF / Airman Rebecca Montez)

F-22A Raptor Demonstration Team aircraft maintainers prepare to launch Maj. Paul "Max" Moga, the first F-22A Raptor demonstration team pilot, on 13 July 2007. The current Raptor demonstration pilot is Major Henry "Schadow" Schantz. (USAF / Senior Airman Christopher L. Ingersoll)

Maj. Paul "Max" Moga, the first F-22A Raptor Demonstration Team Pilot, does a max climb seconds after takeoff during an aircraft demonstration 13 July 2007. The F-22 Demo Team currently consists of six pilots (a lead pilot and five Safety Observers), plus 12 enlisted maintainers. (USAF / Staff Sgt. Samuel Rogers)

A Raptor fires a heat-seeking AIM-9M Sidewinder missile at an enemy aircraft. Sidewinders are carried in the F-22 side bays only. The launch sequence of opening the doors, firing the missile and closing the doors occurs in seconds. The AIM-9M is the latest version of the venerable Sidewinder and is capable of all-aspect target acquisition. It also has a smokeless motor and is capable of defeating infrared countermeasures.

The HGU-86/P helmet used by F-22 pilots reduces the stresses on a pilot's neck by 20 percent during high-speed ejection compared to the current HGU-55/P helmets. The F/A-22 helmet fits more securely as the result of an ear cup tensioning device. The helmet provides improved passive noise protection and incorporates an Active Noise Reduction (ANR) system for enhanced communications. An integrated breathing regulator/anti-g valve (BRAG) controls flow and pressure to the oxygen mask and pressure garments, and the upper body counterpressure garment and a lower body anti-g garment act as a partial pressure suit at high altitudes. The suit is designed for pilots who embark upon missions over cold bodies of water or into chemical/biological warfare. In addition to protection against immersion in cold-water, the suit offers flame protection, protection against chemical/biological-warfare agents, and ventilation.

An F-15E Strike Eagle and an F-22 Raptor fly over the coast of Prince William Sound, Alaska. Both aircraft are from Elmendorf Air Force Base. The 90th Fighter Squadron converted from the Eagle to the Raptor in 2007. (USAF / TSgt Keith. Brown)

Echoing the Cold War, a 90th Fighter Squadron F-22A Raptor escorts a Russian Tu-95 "Bear" bomber flying near the Alaskan NORAD Region airspace on 22 November 2007. It was the first time a Raptor was called upon to support the ANR mission. (USAF)

Raptors from Edwards AFB, Eglin AFB, Tyndall AFB, and Langley AFB on the flightline at Nellis AFB, Nevada, on 6 December 2005. (Lockheed Martin)

Col. Jeff Harrigian, 49th Fighter Wing commander, and Lt. Col. Mike Hernandez, 7th Fighter Squadron commander, fly over White Sands National Monument on the way to their home base, Holloman Air Force Base, New Mexico. (USAF / Senior Airman Russell Scalf)

F-15C and E Eagles fly formation on an F-22A Raptor and an A-10 Thunderbolt II over Tucson, Arizona, on 5 March 2006, during the 2006 Heritage Conference. The conference combines different U.S. aircraft from more than 60 years of aviation history to ensure certification in performing air shows worldwide. (USAF / Airman 1st Class Veronica Pierce)

These two Raptors from the 3rd Wing at Elmendorf Air Force Base, Alaska, are among more than 120 aircraft participating in Northern Edge 2008, the largest military training exercise in Alaska, on 8 May 2008. Aircrews trained in counter-air, close air support and air-interdiction missions. (USAF / TSgt. Mikal Canfield)

Crew chief Staff Sgt. Adam Murtishaw of the 27th Aircraft Maintenance Unit guides an F-22A Raptor into its parking space after a mission. The intake ramps on the Raptor are located within the intake. This configuration, which hides the intake ramps from radar returns, enhances the stealth characteristics of the F-22 aircraft. (USAF /TSgt. Ben Bloker)

Raptor In Service

On 15 December 2005, USAF announced that the F-22 had reached initial operational capability (IOC). The Raptor was then certified ready for employment in combat or in homeland defense missions and was supported by a properly trained and equipped force. The first combat-ready Raptors were assigned to the 27th Fighter Squadron at Langley AFB, Virginia. At the same time, USAF also announced that it was reverting to the aircraft's original F-22A designation instead of F/A-22. The more precise designation is F-22A, with the "A" denoting the first model configuration. Future significant upgrades would result in a model change, such as F-22B or F-22C, assuming the decision to stop production is eventually reversed.

The Air Force completed follow-on test and evaluation (FOT&E) for the F-22 in January 2006, making the Raptor mission capable. While FOT&E was conducted by the Air Force Operational Test and Evaluation Center at Kirtland AFB, New Mexico, most of the actual testing took place at Nellis AFB, Nevada. The tests evaluated the capability of Raptor pilots to employ the GBU-32 Joint Direct Attack Munition (JDAM), and results indicated that the F-22 performed better that it had in the initial operational test and evaluation at Edwards AFB, California, in 2003 and 2004. The F-22 was rated "overwhelmingly effective" in its air-to-air performance during IOT&E.

On 12 December, a Raptor pilot flying at supersonic speed dropped the first guided 1,000-pound GBU-32 Joint Direct Attack Munition on the range at the Air Force Flight Test Center at Edwards AFB, California. This mission was the last major milestone recorded for the F-22 while still designated F/A-22. Beginning in July 2005, Raptor pilots flew seven JDAM supersonic separation test missions under a variety of conditions, but this mission was the first in which the JDAM used internal guidance to hit a target. Plans were made to expand the supersonic JDAM envelope with drops from increasingly higher altitudes and greater speeds. Small diameter bomb testing from the Raptor also began in 2006.

The 27th Fighter Squadron, 1st Fighter Wing, at Langley AFB, Virginia is the oldest fighter squadron in the U.S. Air Force. It seemed appropriate that the 27th was one of the first F-22 squadrons. It flew the first operational missions with the F-22 Raptor on 21-22 January 2006, flying air defense missions over the continental United States as part of Operation Noble Eagle. Col. Thomas Bergeson and Lt. Col. James Hecker, the 27th FS commander, flew the first F-22 mission.

The 94th Fighter Squadron became the second combat squadron to operate the F-22 Raptor on 3 March 2006. Lt. Col. Dirk Smith, squadron commander, and Maj. Kevin Dolata, squadron assistant director of operations, flew Raptors 04-4062 and 04-4063 from Lockheed Martin in Marietta, Georgia, to the 1st FW base at Langley AFB, Virginia. Two new F-22s each month were expected to be delivered to the 94th FS, the second oldest fighter unit in the U.S. Air Force, dating back to World War I. (The "Hat In The Ring" 94th was the unit in which Eddie Rickenbacker became the highest scoring American ace of World War I.)

The 71st FS, the 1st Fighter Wing's third squadron, remained an F-15 unit. The 43rd

Lt. Col. James Hecker (front) and Lt. Col. Evan Dertein line up their F/A-22 Raptors while *en route* to Hill Air Force Base, Utah. Colonel Hecker commanded the first operational Raptor squadron, the 27th Fighter Squadron, at Langley Air Force Base, Virginia. The unit went to Hill AFB for operation Combat Hammer, the squadron's first deployment. The deployment had a twofold goal: complete a deployment and generate a combat-effective sortie rate away from home. (USAF / TSgt Ben Bloker)

The first of 12 F-22 Raptors lands for a brief layover at Hickam Air Force Base, Hawaii, on 7 February 2007. The F-22s and more than 250 Airmen from the 27th Fighter Squadron at Langley Air Force Base, Virginia, are bound for Kadena Air Base, Okinawa, Japan, for the aircraft's first overseas operational deployment. The Raptors are fitted with 600-gallon external tanks under each wing for the long ferry flights. Four hardpoints under the wings can carry up to 5,000 lbs. each. (USAF / TSgt. Shane A. Cuomo)

Fighter Squadron at Tyndall AFB, Florida, the F-22 Raptor training squadron, reached the 5,000-flying-hour mark collectively on 20 September 2006. Tyndall is the second base to achieve the 5,000-hour milestone with the Raptor. The Air Force Flight Test Center at Edwards AFB, California, was the first. The first Tyndall mission took place 31 October 2003, and the 43rd increased its annual flying hours every year after that milestone. In fiscal year 2006, the 43rd F-22s flew 2,770 hours, a fifty percent increase over FY05.

The National Aeronautic Association named the F-22 Raptor aircraft team as the 2006 recipient of the Robert J. Collier Trophy. The award focused on the Raptor's performance in the demanding large-scale Northern Edge joint exercise held in July 2006. During this large-scale exercise, Raptor pilots flew 97 percent of their scheduled missions, achieved an 80:1 kill ratio against the Red Air opponents, scored direct hits with 100 percent of their satellite-guided 1,000-lb. GBU-32 Joint Direct Attack Munitions, and increased overall situational awareness for the entire Blue Force through the F-22's integrated avionics.

The NAA is the oldest national aviation organization in the United States, and many regard the Collier Trophy to be America's most prestigious award for aeronautical and space development. It was established in 1911 and is awarded each year for "the greatest achievement in aeronautics or astronautics in America." The Raptor Team included the Air Force, Lockheed Martin, Boeing, Pratt & Whitney, Northrop Grumman, Raytheon, BAE Systems, and some 1,000 suppliers in 42 states.

Another milestone was reached when the 411th Flight Test Squadron at the Air Force Flight Test Center at Edwards AFB, California, began integration testing of the F-22 and the GBU-39 Small Diameter Bomb, or SDB, in February 2007. The 250-pound class GBU-39 is a low-cost, standoff, next-generation, precision-strike weapon guided by an inertial navigation system with global positioning system updates. Integrating the F-22's stealth and speed and the autonomous standoff capability of the GBU-39 enables the Raptor pilot to release an SDB more than 60 nautical miles from the target. For this close-support mission, the F-22 can carry eight SDBs and two AIM-120 AMRAAM air-to-air missiles in its internal weapons bay.

In a continuation of cold war scenarios, two Russian Tu-95 Bear-H bombers were intercepted close to the U.S. coastline on 22 November 2007 and escorted by two F-22 pilots from the 90th Fighter Squadron at Elmendorf AFB, Alaska. This operational intercept is the first in Raptor history. The North American Aerospace Defense Command (NORAD) Alaskan Regional headquarters launched the Raptors as well as E-3 airborne warning and control assets and a tanker to positively identify and monitor the bombers. After a decade in which no Russian bombers had flown these types of mission, then Russian President Vladimir Putin ordered the resumption of regular long-range bomber patrols by the Russian Air Force to the U.S. and European coastlines in 2007.

The 192nd Fighter Wing closed out its 16-year history flying the F-16 Fighting Falcon with a final four-ship training mission from its base at Richmond International Airport on 20 June 2007. The Virginia Air National Guard unit then officially began operations as a Guard Associate unit at Langley AFB, in Hampton, Virginia, flying the F-22 Raptor.

U.S. Air Force Gen. John D. W. Corley, commander of Air Combat Command,

A crew chief of the 90th Aircraft Maintenance Unit signals the pilot of an F-22 Raptor laden with practice bombs to begin his departure for a training mission at Elmendorf Air Force Base, Alaska. (USAF / Senior Airman Garrett Hothan)

declared on 12 December 2007 that the F-22 Raptor had reached full operational capability. The announcement means the integrated active duty 1st Fighter Wing and Air National Guard 192nd Fighter Wing team at Langley AFB, Virginia, possesses sufficient Raptors, equipment, and trained Airmen to be combat capable and deployable.

Though the Raptor had long-since been declared fully operational, combat capabilities continued to improve through achievement of more milestones. Two F-22 Raptors successfully sent and received data while linked to ground stations in the U.S. Air Force's Joint Expeditionary Force Experiment 2008, or JEFX 08, conducted in April at Nellis AFB, Nevada. During this two-week experiment, two specially configured F-22s were used to transmit real-time sensor information to ground stations at Nellis and at Langley AFB, Virginia, using an experimental version of the Tactical Targeting Network Technology waveform. The F-22 datalink test configuration flew in realistic scenarios that highlighted the Raptor's significant nontraditional intelligence surveillance and reconnaissance capabilities. JEFX is an Air Force Chief of Staff air and ground forces simulation, featuring technology insertions into a warfighting environment.

The Air Force Reserve Command officially activated its first F-22 Raptor unit, the 302nd Fighter Squadron, in ceremonies at Elmendorf AFB, Alaska, on 3 October 2007. The 302nd, which traces its lineage back to the Tuskegee Airmen in World War II, will serve as a Reserve Associate unit of the reactivated 477th Fighter Group. The second active duty F-22 squadron, the 525th Fighter Squadron, was activated at Elmendorf on 29 October. The 525th, which formed in 1942, moved around Europe in its early days but settled at Bitburg AB, Germany, where it stayed for thirty-five years before being inactivated several years ago.

The U.S. Air Force's 82nd Training Wing opened a state-of-the-art, 120,000-square foot F-22 maintenance training facility at Sheppard AFB, Texas, on 19 October 2007. The new facility provided a realistic training environment for future Raptor maintainers. For instructional purposes, engineers have divided the aircraft into seven full-scale, high-fidelity training devices that replicate flight line maintenance conditions and eliminate the need to train on operational aircraft. The devices provide hands-on practice in inspection, operation, removal and installation, system-testing, and fault isolation. The devices range from simple to highly complex, covering as few as fourteen separate tasks to as many as 240 tasks. Boeing served as the design lead on the new facility.

Eight F-22 Raptors and 132 Airmen deployed from Elmendorf AFB, Alaska, to Tyndall AFB, Florida, in February 2008 to participate in Operation Combat Archer, a Weapons System Evaluation Program exercise. This deployment was the first for members of the 3rd Wing and Air Force Reserve Command's 477th Fighter Group, the Reserve Associate unit at the base near Anchorage. Combat Archer evaluates an operational fighter squadron's readiness for combat operations by assessing all phases of its combat operations from weapons loading, to aircraft performance, to aircrew performance. The exercise, which is unique to the U.S. Air Force, is the only test or evaluation program that uses operational aircrews, maintainers, aircraft, and weapons.

In March, 2008, USAF began training new fighter pilots on the Raptor. Previous to this, only experienced F-16 and F-15 pilots were assigned to the Raptor. After lead-in fighter training at Luke AFB, the new F-22 pilots began their Raptor training with the 433rd FS at Tyndall AFB, Florida. These pilots are the first in the Air Force to have the F-22 as their first operational aircraft rather than transitioning to the Raptor from another fighter. The course syllabus included approximately ninety hours of simulator training, twenty-seven academic tests, and more than sixty hours of flight training. The new Raptor pilots graduated on 1 November and completed mission qualification training at their operational F-22 squadrons.

On 11 July 2008, an F-22 test pilot with the 411th Flight Test Squadron at Edwards AFB, California, carried out the first supersonic release of a GBU-39 Small Diameter Bomb, or SDB. All previous SDB drops had been at sub-sonic speeds.

The 525th Fighter Squadron at Elmendorf AFB, Alaska, returned home in early March 2009 after an extended deployment to Nellis AFB, Nevada, and Holloman AFB, New Mexico. The squadron participated in a Red Flag exercise while at Nellis and then, because of volcanic activity in Alaska, the squadron extended their deployment and then trained with the 49th Fighter Wing at Holloman. At Red Flag, the 525th was able to complete all 350 scheduled sorties. When the next Red Flag exercise started, a shortage of ramp space at Nellis necessitated the 525th relocating to Holloman, which as in the process of ramping up as the third operational F-22 base.

The capabilities of the Raptor have changed the persona of the fighter pilot dramatically. When I first started visiting active-duty fighter squadrons in the 1970s, the typical social gathering spot within the squadron was a bar, and many off-duty activities revolved around drinking and raucous (and ribald) games. As the F-15 and F-16s came on the scene, with their ability to sustain high G maneuvers, GLOC became a bigger killer than any enemy force. G-induced Loss Of Consciousness (GLOC) put the focus on the fighter pilots ability to withstand these forces, while getting the most out of his airplane. The squadron bar was quickly replaced or supplanted with a squadron weight room. Aerobic training became almost as important as tactical training, and today the typical fighter pilot is likely to be as buff as any body builder.

The Raptor is magnitudes higher in performance than the fourth generation fighters it has replaced or supplanted. The dangers of that performance were highlighted by the crash of a test F-22. Air Force Materiel Command officials released an accident investigation report that determined that human factors associated with high gravitational forces caused the 25 March 2009 crash of an F-22 test aircraft 35 miles outside of Edwards Air Force Base, Calif.

The test pilot, David Cooley, a Lockheed Martin employee, was killed in the mishap. Mr. Cooley was a former Air Force pilot with significant flight experience, including in the F-22. The aircraft, assigned to the Air Force Flight Test Center at Edwards AFB, was destroyed. Total cost of the aircraft, equipment damage and property restoration has been estimated at $155 million.

According to the report, Mr. Cooley was conducting high-G maneuvers, which test aircraft capabilities and integrated equipment, prior to the accident. Witness statements, voice and telemetry data and simulations show he completed two of three planned tests. During his third test maneuver, however, he appeared to have been subjected to increased

An F-22 Raptor demonstrates its climbing ability during Aviation Nation air show at Nellis Air Force Base, Nevada, in November 2007. Aviation Nation is the Air Force's premier air show and one of the largest in North America. The F-22 is able to sustain supersonic climb at extreme deck angles because of high thrust-to-weight ratios. (A fully-loaded Raptor weighs in at 65,000 lbs, while the twin F-119 engines develop 70,000 lbs. of thrust in afterburner.) (USAF / Master Sgt. Robert W. Valenca)

physiological stressors associated with high-G maneuvers, according to the report.

The board concluded this led to an "almost" loss of consciousness and lack of situational awareness, causing Mr. Cooley to delay his aircraft recovery maneuver.

The report states, "The [mission test pilot] regained partial [situational awareness] and attempted a late recovery from the test maneuver but determined there was inadequate altitude for a safe recovery and ejected."

Due to the speed of the aircraft and the windblast, the pilot immediately sustained fatal, blunt force trauma injuries upon ejection.

The accident board concluded that the aircraft itself was functioning normally and that there were no design or airworthiness issues that would impact the safe operation of the F-22 fleet.

On 21 December 2009, the 8th Fighter Squadron, 49th Fighter Wing, received the first of its 20 F-22 Raptors at Holloman AFB, New Mexico. The 8th had previously flown the F-117, which was retired in April 2008. The squadron history dates to WWII.

On 31 December 2009, USAF announced that fifteen F-22 Raptors were scheduled to deploy to Andersen Air Force Base, Guam, in January 2010 for approximately three months. The Raptors and associated personnel deployed from the 90th Fighter Squadron at Elmendorf AFB, Alaska.

The deployment supported U.S. Pacific Command's theater security packages in the Western Pacific. It followed the recent departure from the theater of two deployed squadrons of F-22s that also were supporting U.S. PACOM's TSP. The fighters and personnel deployed to Andersen AFB, Guam, and Kadena Air Base, Japan, completed their redeployment in October 2009.

A U.S. Air Force F-22 Raptor returns to Kadena Air Base, Okinawa, Japan, following a mission on 16 January 2009. The Raptor was deployed from the 27th Fighter Squadron, based at Langley Air Force Base, Virginia. (USAF / Master Sgt. Andy Dunaway)

A Raptor prepares for aerial refueling, its Xar-built air refueling receptacle visible on the top side of the aircraft in the mid-fuselage directly behind the cockpit. It is covered by two butterfly doors that have integral low-voltage lights to aid in night refueling. (Lockheed Martin)

Members of the 3rd Logistics Readiness Squadron ensure an F-22 Raptor is refueled properly during a hot pit refuel at Elmendorf Air Force Base, Alaska, on 1 September 2009. During hot pit refuels, the pilot pulls the aircraft up to the area without shutting down the engines, the plane is quickly refueled, and can immediately take off. (USAF / Airman 1st Class Christopher Gross)

F-22 Raptors provided strike packages of better aircraft spherical situational awareness when they pulled their first Air Expeditionary Force duty in 2007. The 27th Fighter Squadron at Langley Air Force Base, Virginia, was scheduled to fly the first Raptors in combat. (USAF / Senior Airman Austin Knox)

Maj. Dave Skalicky roars by the crowd in full afterburner during the Air Power over Hampton Roads air show at Langley Air Force Base, Virginia, on 26 April 2009. The F119 engines develop more than twice the thrust of current engines under supersonic conditions, and more thrust without afterburner than conventional engines with afterburner. (USAF / Senior Airman Vernon Young)

An F-22 Raptor shows transonic shock waves as it performs a supersonic flyby over the aircraft carrier USS *John C. Stennis* during Exercise Northern Edge 2009, a joint exercise in Alaska focusing on detecting and tracking units at sea, in the air, and on land. Northern Edge is the premier exercise carried out within the area of responsibility of the U.S. Pacific Command. (U.S. Navy / Petty Officer 1st Class Ronald Dejarnett)

Lt. Col. Craig Baker exits the first F-22 Raptor assigned to the 8th Fighter Squadron after flying it to Holloman Air Force Base, New Mexico, on 21 December 2009. The history of the 8th FS Black Sheep began in 1941 when the squadron was assigned to the 49th Pursuit Group. Colonel Baker is the 8th Fighter Squadron commander. (USAF / Senior Airman John D. Strong II)

A Raptor makes a high-speed flyby during an airshow performance. A testament to the sometimes counter intuitive computer-controlled flight controls is the upward deflection of both ailerons in a left turn. (Lockheed Martin)

The Vehicle Management System (VMS) provides integrated flight and propulsion control and facilitates maneuvers like the one shown here. The VMS lets the pilot maneuver the F-22 to its maximum capabilities. The VMS includes the control stick, throttle, rudder pedals and actuators, air data probes, accelerometers, leading edge flap drive actuators, and the primary flight control actuators. (Lockheed Martin)

When they participate in airshows, Raptor pilots routinely display their aircraft's extremely high angle of attack maneuvers, which deliver dramatic atmospheric effects. The F-22 has a service ceiling of 60,000 feet, but unlike other current fighters, the Raptor is entirely capable of performing tactical maneuvers even at this altitude. (Lockheed Martin)

An F-22 Raptor from the 412th Test Wing of The Air Force Flight Test Center, Edwards AFB, flies a training mission over the painted California desert on 28 March 2005. The F-22 Combined Test Force is based at Edwards. (USAF)

F-22A 91-4005 is a Block 10 Raptor, delivered to the USAF on 1 January 2001. It was used as the test aircraft for Integrated avionics, radar, CNI, and armament before being transferred to the 1st FW in 2005. (Lockheed Martin)

Both the 91-4005 and 91-4007 flying wing, carry the Edwards AFB tail code. 4007 was delivered on 1 October 2001 and served as the test aircraft for integrated avionics and air vehicle performance for the 411th Flight Test Squadron. (Lockheed Martin)

The Raptor's Future

In April 2009, Secretary of Defense Robert Gates announced that the F-22 Raptor production run would end at 187 aircraft, with the last Raptor projected to roll off the assembly line in 2011. The original production run was initially set at 740 aircraft, and later scaled back to 383 aircraft.

If it is true that the Generals always fight the last war, then it would seem they are committed to fighting a war against irregular forces well into the future. The F-22 was envisioned as the ultimate air superiority fighter against a large enemy force of sophisticated aircraft. It was designed, built, and has evolved as the best air superiority fighter in history. Along the way, it acquired the capability to deliver precision-guided munitions from long range, while remaining virtually invisible to enemy radars.

Irregular forces, such as those the U.S. has faced in Iraq and Afghanistan, do not have air defense radars or sophisticated surface-to-air missiles. They do not have any air-to-air fighters either. They do have a seemingly endless supply of individuals who are anxious to kill Americans, military or civilian, while sacrificing themselves on the altar of "martyrdom." Sending a $130 million airplane out to drop a bomb on a dozen irregulars is several magnitudes of overkill, which is why, to date, no Raptors have flown combat missions in either of these theatres.

In a *Washington Post* op-ed piece, published on 13 April 2009, Secretary of the Air Force Michael Donley and Air Force Chief of Staff Gen. Norton Schwartz explained the rationalization for terminating the F-22 program by citing the constraints of a fixed Defense budget. In their words; "Buying more F-22s means doing less of something else." The biggest "something else" on the immediate horizon is the F-35 Strike Fighter. Did I say that the Generals always fight the last war? It turns out that the defense establishment is also guilty of procurement redux.

More than 30 years ago, it was the F-15 proponents fighting for more air superiority capability against the lightweight fighter F-16 advocates. Both fighters turned out to be extremely successful on the world-wide stage. The F-15 has never been bested in aerial combat, and the F-16 has evolved into one of the most potent universal fighters ever built, primarily as an air-to-ground platform. Given the variables involved in that mission, the F-16 program has been a much longer and more lucrative procurement program than the F-15. The innovative design of the F-16 allowed the aircraft to grow in complexity and capability, contributing to the longevity of the program.

Given its demonstrated capability against both the F-15 and F-16 in simulated combat exercises, it seems a safe bet that the Raptor will be to the 21st century what the F-15 was to the last century. Whether the F-35 will be as successful as the F-16 remains to be seen, but the decision to stop production of the Raptor in 2011 indicates that the generals and defense industry officials are confident that the F-35 Lightning II will supplant the F-16. Unless defense budgets are somehow dramatically increased in the near future, it is highly unlikely that there will be more Raptors built beyond 2011.

Whether the Raptor will be as dominant in the air-to-air arena as the F-15 is also an open question. On 29 January 2010, the Russians flew their first fifth-generation fighter. The Sukhoi T-50, which made its first flight from Komsomol'sk-na-Amure in Russia's Far East, is the first aircraft completely designed and built in Russia since the break-up of the Soviet Union. It is an outgrowth of the Multi-function fighter program begun by the Mikoyan Design Bureau in 1981, but it languished undeveloped as the Soviet Union disintegrated. The T-50 is similar in size to the Su-27 (dubbed the "Flanker" by NATO) and Russian sources indicate that, like the Raptor, the T-50 has super cruise capability and stealth characteristics.

The T-50 was developed in partnership with the Indian Air Force, and it seems likely that production of the T-50 will exceed 187 aircraft. Although full production and operational capability will take several years to realize, when the T-50 is finally operational, the Raptor will have a worthy counterpart, and possible adversary.

Maj. Kevin Dolata, an F-15 Eagle pilot from the 1st Fighter Wing, and Maj. Charles Corcoran, an F/A-22 Raptor pilot assigned to the 27th Fighter Squadron, fly in formation *en route* to a training area off the coastline of Virginia on 5 April 2005. The 27th Fighter Squadron is performing regular operations with two Raptors on loan from Tyndall Air Force Base, Florida. While the Raptor and Eagle share similar aerodynamic characteristics, the stealthiness of the F-22 is accentuated by its uncluttered lines, while the F-15 is literally a flying radar return because of the plethora of external stores and hardpoints. (USAF / TSgt Ben Bloker)

Two Raptors fly over the Pacific after refueling on 9 March 2009. The F22s deployed from Elmendorf Air Force Base, Alaska, to the 90th Expeditionary Fighter Squadron at Andersen Air Force Base, Guam. While deployed, the fighters and associated maintenance and support personnel underwent routine training in an environment different from their home station. (USAF / Master Sgt. Kevin J. Gruenwald)

An F/A-22 Raptor taxis after landing at Hill AFB, Utah. The jet, from the 27th Fighter Squadron at Langley Air Force Base, was deployed for the next-generation fighter's first deployment for live-weapons bomb-training exercise. (USAF / Staff Sgt. Samuel Rogers)

A test Raptor carries four Small-Diameter Bombs in its main weapons bay on 2 February 2007, as pilots and engineers of the F-22 Combined Test Force perform load tests to ensure the GBU-39/B Small Diameter Bomb system does not exceed structural load limits for the Raptor. (Darin Russell)

The F-22 Raptor demonstration team performed during an air show at Naval Base Ventura County in Point Mugu, California. The F-22 was based at Langley Air Force Base, Virginia. Advanced flight controls, thrust vectoring, and high thrust-to-weight ratio provide the capability to outmaneuver all current and projected adversary aircraft. (USAF / TSgt Justin D. Pyle)

Airman 1st Class Shawn Krause and Staff Sgt. Justin Speak prepare to launch an F-22 Raptor at Tyndall AFB, Florida. (USAF / Scott Wolfe)

Staff Sgt. Charlie Grantham prepares to launch an F-22 Raptor at Tyndall Air Force Base, Florida. Members of the 3rd Wing and Air Force Reserve Command's 477th Fighter Group from Elmendorf AFB, Alaska, combined for its first F-22 Raptor deployment to Tyndall AFB for Combat Archer. (USAF / Scott Wolfe)

Senior Airman Kurtis Toycen, a fuels specialist with the 49th Logistics Readiness Squadron at Holloman Air Force Base, New Mexico, secures a refueling hose while Tech. Sgt. Aaron Cowan, a maintainer with the 49th Aircraft Maintenance Squadron, locks the fuel receptacle on an F-22 Raptor. The team successfully refueled the aircraft while its engines were still running, a procedure called "hot refueling." The single-point refueling receptacle requires a large-diameter hose. (USAF / Airman 1st Class Jamal D. Sutter)

An F/A-22, flown by Maj. John Teichert, releases a guided bomb unit-32 1,000-pound joint direct attack munitions at supersonic speed for the first time near California's Panamint Mountain range. Major Teichert is a test pilot assigned to the 411th Flight Test Squadron at Edwards Air Force Base, California. (USAF / Darin Russell)

F-22 Raptor 4002 fires an AIM-9 Sidewinder air-to-air missile during a separation test at 40,000 feet. Flown at a 26-degree angle-of-attack at only Mach .4 speed, the test flight demonstrated the Raptor's ability to operate at slow speeds in a combat environment and still maintain maneuverability. (Judson Brohmer)

A weapons load team from the 27th Aircraft Maintenance Unit loads 20mm rounds on an F-22A Raptor during a Phase 1 operational readiness exercise. Weapons loaders are practicing load configurations to assess the time it takes to fully load the aircraft. The Phase 1 ORE is an evaluation of the base's ability to prepare and deploy personnel, equipment, and support assets to a combat environment. (USAF / TSgt. Ben Bloker)

The Raptor's unique shape contributes to its "stealthiness," but another, less publicized stealth feature is a new type of paint that increases the Raptor stealthiness by reducing its vulnerability to infrared threats. To meet these requirements, Boeing developed a topcoat that protects the aircraft against a broad range of wavelengths and replaces conventional topcoats. The characteristics that enhance stealth do not compromise protection against the elements. While the new paint does not add to the F-22's weight, its slick surface enhances performance at a very modest cost. The two-tone camouflage design is patterned after the F-15 "Mod-Eagle" paint scheme. Development of the new paint began early in the F-22 program. The team at Boeing in Seattle refined the paint and improved its application characteristics at the production-level. Technicians at Lockheed Martin painted the first few aircraft by hand. Robotic application is planned for future Raptors. Application of the topcoat is expected to take one or two days for each Raptor. Gray became the dominant camouflage scheme during the 1970s, when experimental schemes were tried with various colors and hues. "Air Superiority Blue" was meant to blend into a blue sky and was applied to the first F-15 Eagles. Unfortunately, this scheme only seemed to enhance visual acquisition of the Eagles. Most artists know that distance diminishes the intensity of colors, eventually causing them to become more gray and indistinct. Gray camouflage schemes are singularly uninteresting, but they are also the most effective camouflage in air-to-air situations.

Employees at the Lockheed Martin Aeronautics Company assembly plant in Marietta, Georgia, paint the first operational F/A-22 Raptor to be delivered to the Air Force. The jet, Raptor 18, will be used to train pilots in the 43rd Fighter Squadron at Tyndall Air Force Base, Florida. One aircraft is expected to reach Tyndall each month following Raptor 18's arrival. (USAF /John Rossino)

Employees at Lockheed Martin's F-22A Raptor production facility here attach a tail fin to the body of Raptor 4087. The aircraft, the first to bear the "AK" tail flash, is destined for Elmendorf Air Force Base, Alaska. (Lockheed-Martin)

Workers at Lockheed Martin's F-22A production facility assemble Raptor 4087. The first of 36 Raptors to be assigned to Pacific Air Forces, the aircraft is headed for Elmendorf Air Force Base in Alaska. (Lockheed-Martin)

Staff Sgt. Jeremiah Smith, left, and Senior Airman Theodore Cupp, crew chiefs with the 525th Expeditionary Aircraft Maintenance Unit, work on the system-one hydraulic pump beneath a Raptor at Andersen Air Force Base in Guam. The Airmen deployed from Elmendorf Air Force Base, Alaska, in support of the Theater Security Package. (USAF / Sr. Airman Christopher Bush)

Sr. Airmen Idma Ramirez and Sheila Smith, both crew chiefs with the 90th Aircraft Maintenance Unit, Elmendorf Air Force Base, Alaska, inspect an F-22 during exercise Red Flag 11-3 at Nellis Air Force Base, Nevada. (DoD / TSgt. Michael R. Holzworth)

Airman 1st Class Daniel Kok, a weapons loader with the 36th Expeditionary Maintenance Squadron, conducts a preflight inspection of an F-22 Raptor aircraft at Andersen Air Force Base in Guam on 15 April 2009. The 90th Fighter Squadron, based at Elmendorf Air Force Base, Alaska, was on a three-month deployment to Andersen as part of a theater security package. (USAF / Master Sgt. Kevin J. Gruenwald)

Raptor 18, the first operational F/A-22 to be delivered to the Air Force, sits on the ramp at Tyndall Air Force Base near Panama City in Florida, as a ground crew checks the plane. (USAF / Lisa Carroll)

Lt. Col. John Hillyer conducts preflight checks on his F-22 Raptor stealth fighter during Exercise Northern Edge 09 at Elmendorf Air Force Base, Alaska, on 17 June 2009. Northern Edge, Alaska's largest military training exercise, prepares joint forces to respond to crises throughout the Asia-Pacific region. (USAF / Master Sgt. Shane A. Cuomo)

One of the test points for the Raptor was the ability to carry and launch weapons from external hardpoints. This F-22 carries a pair of AIM-120 missiles on external launchers. Normal combat configuration would not include any external stores, since they would compromise stealth capability. (Lockheed Martin)

Capt. Ryan Owen, a 49th Fighter Wing F-22 Raptor pilot, performs preflight checks before a training mission at the Nevada Test and Training Range during Red Flag 11-3 at Nellis Air Force Base, on 1 March 2011. Red Flag is an advanced aerial combat training exercise held four to six times a year to train pilots from the U.S., NATO and other allied countries for real combat situations. (USAF / Senior Airman Brett Clashman)

Lt. Col. John Hillyer prepares for a mission in the cockpit of his F-22 Raptor stealth fighter during Exercise Northern Edge 09 at Elmendorf Air Force Base, Alaska, on 17 June 2009. (USAF / Master Sgt. Shane A. Cuomo)

On the ramp of the 128th Air Refueling Wing, an F-22 Raptor assigned to the Air Combat Command Air Demonstration Team prepares for its chance to take to the air during the Milwaukee Air and Water Show on Thursday, 10 June 2010. This Raptor is one of a pair that travels throughout the world to promote the U.S. Air Force and showcase the superiority of the USAF's most advanced fighter aircraft. (USAF / Staff Sgt. Jeremy Wilson)

Two F-22 Raptors and a B-2 Spirit bomber deployed to Andersen Air Force Base in Guam, fly in formation over the Pacific Ocean. The deployment to Andersen marks the first time F-22s and B-2s, the key strategic stealth assets in the Air Force inventory, deployed together outside the continental United States. (USAF / Master Sgt. Kevin J. Gruenwald)

A U.S. Air Force F-22 Raptor aircraft assigned to the 90th Fighter Squadron, Elmendorf Air Force Base, Alaska, flies near Guam on 17 February 2010. (USAF / Staff Sgt. Andy M. Kin)

An F-22 Raptor is refueled while participating in Valiant Shield at Andersen Air force Base in Guam. Valiant Shield is an integrated joint training exercise that allows different units and teams from across the military the opportunity to work together. (USAF / Airman Julian North)

Lt. Col. Bryan Salmon, 149th Fighter Squadron director of operations, readies an F-22 Raptor for taxiing during an Operational Readiness Inspection at Langley Air Force Base, Virginia, on 10 April 2011. The inspection evaluates an installation's ability to deploy military members, cargo, and equipment efficiently while adjusting to rapidly changing security conditions. (USAF / Airman 1st Class Teresa Zimmerman)

A three-ship formation of F-22 Raptors flies to the Nevada Test and Training Range during the Red Flag exercise on 4 February 2010. Red Flag is a realistic combat training exercise involving the air forces of the United States and its allies. The Raptors are from the 90th Fighter Squadron at Elmendorf Air Base, Alaska, and the 49th Fighter Wing at Holloman AFB, New Mexico. (USAF / Staff Sgt. Taylor Worley)

Clockwise from left, an F-22 Raptor, a propeller-driven P-51 Mustang fighter, an F-4 Phantom jet, and an F-86 Sabre jet take part in the Air Combat Command Heritage Flight during the 2010 Aviation Nation open house at Nellis Air Force Base in Nevada on 12 November 2010. (USAF / Airman 1st Class Daniel Hughes)

An F-22 Raptor in the foreground, and an F-15 Eagle assigned to the U.S. Air Force Weapons School, 433rd Weapons Squadron, Nellis Air Force Base, go into a vertical climb during training at the Nevada Test and Training Range on 16 July 2010. The school provides the most advanced training in weapons and tactics employment. (USAF / Master Sgt. Kevin J. Gruenwald)

An F/A-22 Raptor, a vintage F-4 Phantom II, and a propeller-driven P-51 Mustang conduct a heritage fly-over during the Aviation Nation 2005 air show at Nellis Air Force Base, Nevada. (USAF / TSgt. Demetrius Lester)

Demonstrating the proud legacy of 60 years of U.S. military aviation, a P-38 Lightning of the Army Air Forces and an Air Force F-22 Raptor take part in a heritage flight at Offutt Air Force Base in Nebraska on 28 August 2010. (USAF / Josh Plueger)

An F-22 Raptor goes over the top in a loop. The Raptor's rate of climb is still officially classified, but test flights have demonstrated that it exceeds that of the F-15 Eagle, even though the Eagle has a greater thrust-to-weight ratio. (Lockheed Martin)

Four F-22 Raptors of the Operational Test and Evaluation Squadron fly a perfect echelon over Edwards AFB, California. The first crash of an F-22 took place near Edwards on 26 March 2009. Veteran Lockheed Martin test pilot David Cooley was killed in the accident. Cooley had joined Lockheed Martin after a 21-year career in the U.S. Air Force. Cooley had racked up 121 flight hours in the Raptor at the time of the accident, which investigators attributed to loss of control during high-g maneuvers testing. Partial incapacitation of the pilot led to late recovery procedures, including ejection from the aircraft at high speed and low altitude. (Lockheed Martin)

Three U.S. Air Force F-22 Raptors assigned to the 49th Fighter Wing, Holloman Air Force Base, New Mexico, fly over the Nevada Test and Training Range during a Red Flag 11-3 training mission on 2 March 2011. Red Flag brings together U.S. and allied air force personnel for combat training. (USAF / Senior Airman Brett Clashman)

Lt. Col. John Hillyer climbs into the cockpit of his F-22 stealth fighter during Exercise Northern Edge 09 at Elmendorf Air Force Base, Alaska, on 17 June 2009. (USAF / Master Sgt. Shane A. Cuomo)

An F-22 Raptor of the 1st Fighter Wing makes a high-speed, high-G, low-altitude pass at a September 2010 demonstration. Various sources have indicated that the F-22 is capable of sustained turns of 9.5G, and that a new full-body G-suit worn by the pilots enables them to resist or delay the onset of G-Induced Loss of Consciousness (GLOC). (David F. Brown)

The complete absence of traditional pressure instruments such as airspeed, altitude, and attitude instruments in the operational F-22 cockpit is a testament to the reliability of computer-generated displays. The Raptor has a side-stick controller, like that found in the F-16, while the throttles are in the conventional left console location. (Lockheed Martin)

The chaff and flares dispensers on the Raptor are just behind the side missile bays. The F-22 ejects chaff and/or flare decoys to evade missile attacks. Chaff decoys confuse radar images to divert radar-guided missiles, while flare decoys provide a brilliant heat/light source to decoy heat-seeking missiles. The F-22 carries 20 chaff packages and 40 flares. (Lockheed Martin)

This overhead view of one of the test Raptors reveals the camouflage pattern applied to the F-22. Also evident is the stealth-enhancing design of most surfaces, which feature serrated or angular edges that deflect radar returns away from the aircraft. (Lockheed Martin)

Each lower missile bay of the F-22 can carry three AIM-120 Advanced Medium Range Air to Air Missiles (AMRAAM). The AMRAAM is a radar-guided missile with a range in excess of 30 miles and a terminal speed of Mach 4. It has scored air-to-air kills in Iraq, Bosnia, and Kosovo. The radar guidance is autonomous, giving the pilot launch and leave capability. (Lockheed Martin)

Each side weapons bay can carry a single AIM-9 Sidewinder missile. The AIM-9M version is loaded in this Raptor. The Sidewinder design dates to the early 1950s. Unlike the original version, the latest Sidewinders have all-aspect acquisition capability, enhanced countermeasures, and smokeless motors that make them difficult to see and/or defeat by target aircraft. (Lockheed Martin)

Senior Airman Marquell Stalling (left) drives an MJ-1, a vehicle specially made to load munitions, as Staff Sgt. Eric Venter guides an AIM-9X missile at Keflavík, Iceland, on 23 September 2010. Sergeant Venter and Airman Stallings are deployed from the 748th Aircraft Maintenance Squadron at Royal Air Force Lakenheath, England. (USAF / Senior Airman Stephen Linch)

A Raptor of the 1st Fighter Wing taxies out on a 19 September 2008 mission. The 1st Fighter Wing was the first air combat unit organized under the U.S. Army air arm as the 1st Pursuit Group at Gencoult, France on 5 May 1918. The Virginia Air National Guard's 192nd Fighter Wing, based at Langley AFB, was the first Air Guard unit to fly the F-22 Raptor in support of Operation Noble Eagle. (The 1st FW and 192nd FW combined in October 2007.) The first active-duty Raptor flight in support of Operation Noble Eagle was flown in January 2007. The 27th FS, 1st FW, was the first unit to conduct an operational flight with live ordnance loaded in the Raptor. (David F. Brown)

A U.S. Air Force F-22 Raptor assigned to the 3rd Fighter Wing flies over the Nevada Test and Training Range near Nellis Air Force Base on a training mission during exercise Red Flag on 3 March 2011. Since 1975, personnel from the U.S. Air Force, other U.S. military services and allied militaries have participated in Red Flag exercises. (USAF / Senior Airman Brett Clashman)

In May 2011 the entire Raptor fleet was grounded due to an investigation into the November 2010 crash of an F-22 in Alaska. As the investigation came to focus on the Raptor's oxygen system, the airplanes were allowed to fly, but restricted to a ceiling of 25,000 feet while the investigation proceeded. The oxygen system was less crucial at lower altitudes where the atmosphere is more oxygen-rich. (David F. Brown)

U.S. Air Force F-22 Raptors assigned to the 90th Fighter Squadron, Elmendorf Air Force Base, Alaska, fly near Guam on 16 February 2010. (USAF / Staff Sgt. Jacob N. Bailey)